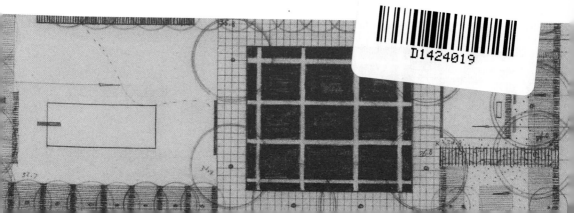

# DANIEL URBAN KILEY
The Early Gardens

William S. Saunders, editor

*with essays by*

Anita Berrizbeitia
Joseph Disponzio
Daniel Donovan
James Marston Fitch
Gary R. Hilderbrand
Mark A. Klopfer

Published by
Princeton Architectural Press
37 East 7th Street
New York, New York 10003
212.995.9620

For a free catalog of books, call 1.800.722.6657
Visit our web site at www.papress.com

Editing and Design: Clare Jacobson
Special thanks to: Eugenia Bell, Jane Garvie, Caroline Green,
Therese Kelly, Mark Lamster, Anne Nitschke, and Sara E.
Stemen of Princeton Architectural Press
—Kevin C. Lippert, publisher

Library of Congress Cataloging-in-Publication Data
Daniel Urban Kiley : the early gardens / William S. Saunders,
editor.
        p. cm. — (Landscape views ; 2)
    Includes bibliographical references.
    ISBN 1-56898-148-1
        1. Kiley, Dan (Dan Urban)  2. Landscape architecture—
United States.  3. Landscape architects—United States—
Biography. I. Harvard University.  Graduate School of Design.
II. Series.
    SB470.K55 D35 1999
    712'.092—dc21
    [B]                                        98-44892
                                        CIP

## About the Contributors

Anita Berrizbeitia is Assistant Professor of Landscape Architecture at the Graduate School of Fine Arts, University of Pennsylvania.

Joseph Disponzio is Assistant Professor of Landscape Architecture at the Harvard University Graduate School of Design. For
many years he was a senior landscape architect for the New
York City Department of Parks and Recreation.

Daniel Donovan was archivist from 1995–7 for the Dan Kiley
collection at the Harvard University Graduate School of Design.
He is an architect and urban designer and teaches in the Landscape Architecture program at Florida A & M University.

James Marston Fitch, Hon. AIA, is Chairperson Emeritus of
Historic Preservation at Beyer Blinder Belle, Architects, New
York. He founded and directed the graduate programs in his-
toric preservation at Columbia University and the University of
Pennsylvania, and is the author of several books.

Gary R. Hilderbrand is an Associate Professor of Landscape
Architecture and Director of the Master in Landscape Architecture degree program at Harvard University Graduate School
of Design.

Mark A. Klopfer is both an architect and landscape architect.
He is a Design Critic in the Landscape Architecture Department
at the Harvard University Graduate School of Design.

William S. Saunders is Editor of Harvard Design Magazine and
Assistant Dean of External Relations at the Harvard University
Graduate School of Design.

For information or proposals, please write to
Landscape Views
c/o Princeton Architectural Press
37 East 7th Street
New York, New York 10003

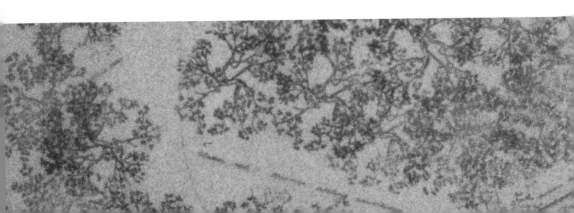

# CONTENTS

# PREFACE

James Marston Fitch

Dan Kiley's first two decades of work are notable in that they reveal both his philosophical commitment to modernist design and his sheer mastery of the medium of landscape architecture from the outset of his career. This book is itself independently significant for the eloquence and perceptive powers of its contributors. Their perspective on Kiley's work is that of a generation that understands and agrees with Kiley's pioneering work in both theory and practice. The careful research and broad experience that underlie each of their papers have resulted in authoritative explorations of key examples of Kiley's work.

In their now-famous manifesto of 1939, Kiley and his collaborators Garret Eckbo and James Rose called for a new definition of landscape architecture. They condemned the Beaux-Arts formalism that had dominated the profession for half a century, and argued that instead of being merely beautiful to look at, the modern landscape had to be satisfactory to be in. This revolutionary doctrine of usefulness/utility as the main criterion in the new landscape design was, in short, the same doctrine as that of the functionalist modernism that was overtaking American architecture at that time. It is indicative of the strength and viability of the Kilean doctrine that it has survived and flourished in the last half century to become the dominant mode of thought and action in the practice of landscape architecture today.

It is a source of great satisfaction to me that, as an editor of *Architectural Record* sixty years ago, I was able to publish this now-historic manifesto that has proved to be one of the basic documents in the history of modern American landscape architecture.

# INTRODUCTION
A New England Yankee in an Internationalist Court


Joseph Disponzio

Daniel Urban Kiley is arguably the most important American landscape architect of the second half of the twentieth century, yet much of his early work—from the late 1930s to the late 1950s—is little known and understood. In November 1997 at the Harvard University Graduate School of Design, an exhibition and symposium meant to redress this unfamiliarity was held; this book grew from those events. The exhibition, which included over 120 drawings from the first two decades of Kiley's career,[1] focused on some of his least-known works and on never-executed plans for some of his best. The essays here (including this one) respond to that work, particularly Kiley's early housing projects and garden prototypes, and his garden plans for the Hollin Hills subdivision in suburban Washington, D.C.

Kiley has not made the task of critically investigating his early career easy—he has made a sport of sparring with the profession that places him at its top, ignoring the professional establishment, writing little, and avoiding explanations of his work. He has never joined its national organization, the American Society of Landscape Architects (ASLA). Yet from rural Vermont, where he has run his office for almost sixty years, he has remained a dominant figure in modern landscape architecture and its discourse.

He is disinclined, if not quietly hostile, to any perceived academic, intellectualized scrutiny of his work. His own biographical construction, anecdotes, and *bons mots* are so often repeated that they are now treated as mythical, virtually beyond critique, and thus problematic for scholarship. While he has been a frequent speaker at American universities since the late 1950s, his discussion of his work is so personal that little concrete understanding of his theory and methods has emerged; the seriously intended essays and articles devoted to his work have seldom succeeded when taking him at his word. If the clarity of his landscapes stands in stark contrast to his sometimes-inscrutable words, the safer critical approach has been to assume no relationship between the two, rather than try to construct their connection. Nor has there been any serious investigation and synthesis of the literary and philosophical sources, from Heraclitus to Carl Jung, that Kiley claims were formative in his thinking.[2] Researchers' near total avoidance of these sources, perhaps abetted by Kiley himself, has

---

1. The exhibited works are part of the Dan Kiley Drawings Archive, housed in the Special Collections of Harvard's Frances Loeb Library. An exhibition checklist is given at the end of this book. Mary Daniels, Head of Special Collections at the Loeb Library, provided invaluable assistance and insight in this endeavor.

2. Scattered about in his published articles or interviews Kiley has mentioned the following influences: Heraclitus, Thomas Jefferson, Henry James, Henry David Thoreau, Ralph Waldo Emerson, Johann Wolfgang von Goethe, Soren Kierkegaard, Carl Jung, Gaston Bachelard, and Laurens van der Post.

weakened and diminished Kiley scholarship.[3]

Dan Kiley was born on 12 September 1912 in the Roxbury section of Boston. Early on he knew that he was going to collaborate with nature in the creation of landscapes. After graduation from Jamaica Plain High School in 1930, he began an unpaid apprenticeship with Warren Manning; eventually he became Manning's associate. Despite Kiley's fond recollections of Manning and the acknowledged debt he owes the elder landscape architect, we know virtually nothing about Kiley's association with Manning. To date we have not one significant work, based on archival evidence or otherwise, from this phase of Kiley's career.[4] Kiley's account that "Warren Manning told me two things: don't go to Harvard, and don't join the ASLA"[5] is too often all that is remembered of these years. It is indeed curious that Manning, one of the founders of the American Society of Landscape Architects and twice its president, should so counsel his young associate. It is even more curious in the context of Manning's professional life. As an employee of Frederick Law Olmsted, Manning was a direct link to the very foundations of the practice, design, and philosophy of the American landscape architecture tradition. Kiley's exposure to Manning and his office linked him with this heritage, only one professional generation removed from its source. Kiley was both witness and participant to the transformation of this heritage. The story of how landscape architecture in America—or at least the branch that Kiley followed—repudiated and abandoned almost a century of practice and tradition has yet to be fully elucidated.[6]

Ignoring Manning's advice, Kiley enrolled in Harvard's Graduate School of Design in 1936 (without having had any undergraduate education). Every student of landscape architecture who has ever heard Kiley speak can lip-sync his recollection of the Harvard years, "At Harvard…my only satisfying course was Music 1."[7] Yet Kiley profited quite a bit from Harvard—if not directly through a rigorous program of study, then through the broader, enriching, academic environment of modern internationalist fervor initiated upon the arrival of Walter Gropius as dean in 1937. Perhaps as important were Kiley's friendships, notably with Garret Eckbo and James Rose, with whom he authored three now-famous essays in *Architectural*

3. See bibliographic note on page 80 of this book.

4. The Warren H. Manning archives are considerable and are distributed in part between the Frances Loeb Library of Harvard University, the University of Massachusetts at Lowell, and Iowa State University.

5. Dan Kiley, "Manning Memoirs" (Charlotte, Vermont: Office of Dan Kiley, 2 October 1987).

6. Recent works—Marc Treib and Dorothy Imbert's *Garret Eckbo: Modern Landscapes for Living* (Berkeley: University of California Press, 1997) and Dean Cardasis's work at the James Rose Center for Landscape Architectural Research and Design, Ridgewood, New Jersey—as well as writings by Eckbo and Rose themselves have added to our understanding of this redirection of the course of American landscape architecture. Nonetheless the story remains incomplete.

7. Dan Kiley, "Nature: The Source of All Design," *Landscape Architecture* (January 1963): 127. Kiley often repeats this quote, in various forms. However, his Harvard transcript indicates no record of credit for any music course.

*Record*, written between 1939 and 1940 at the instigation of *AR*'s editor James Marston Fitch.[8] At Harvard Kiley might have thrived precisely because the historicist academic atmosphere of the landscape architecture curriculum proved so repellent—his career seems to suggest that this situation was conducive to his development. Antagonism is a form of competition, and Dan Kiley is nothing if not a competitor.

Kiley left Harvard in 1938, without completing a degree,[9] and briefly worked in Concord, New Hampshire. Shortly thereafter, he moved to Washington, D.C. to work on public housing for the United States government. His stay in the nation's capital proved crucial: there he met, among others, Louis Kahn and Eero Saarinen, and cultivated friendships with people who would become future clients or would put him in the circles for meeting them. Anita Berrizbeitia, in this volume, begins to sort out the chronology, establish the network of connections, and present for the first time a serious look at his work from this period.

In 1942 Kiley was inducted into the United States Army as a private and quickly became a captain. By his own account, Kiley's army experience was positive. It is ironic that the military, which required strict conformity and regimentation, enabled an independent-minded Kiley to nurture his professional development. His work in the Army Corps of Engineers gave him valuable experience with landscape engineering, surveying, and earth moving. He replaced Eero Saarinen as Chief of the Design Section for the Office of Strategic Services, a position that he recalls with particular satisfaction. The OSS was on par with a "superb private design office, with some of the most talented artists in America."[10] During this period, Kiley conceived and developed design concepts that would reemerge in future work. In one of the rare designs of the era to survive, a 1944 plan for the Air Transport Command Passenger Terminal and Operations Building in Washington, D.C. (fig. 1), Kiley introduced a series of abstract and amorphous planting areas set within rectangular spaces. This schematic idea resurfaced twice—once in the first phase for the Jefferson National Expansion Memorial Competition and again in the Cadet Quadrangle Gardens for the United States Air Force Academy. Neither postwar plan was executed.

8. "Landscape Design in the Urban Environment," *Architectural Record* (May 1939): 70–7; "Landscape Design in the Rural Environment," *Architectural Record* (August 1939): 68–73; and "Landscape Design in the Primeval Environment," *Architectural Record* (February 1940): 74–9. These articles were reprinted in their entirety, without, however, their vintage images, in Marc Treib, ed., *Modern Landscape Architecture: A Critical Review* (Cambridge: MIT Press, 1993), 78–91.

9. "The Work of Dan Kiley: A Dialogue on Design Theory," *Proceedings of the First Annual Symposium on Landscape Architecture* (Charlottesville, Virginia: University of Virginia, 1982), 8. Kiley most probably withdrew from Harvard for financial reasons. Manning had died in February 1936 and his office was being dissolved. Throughout his Harvard years, Kiley worked in Manning's office.

10. Dan Kiley, "Preparations for History's Greatest Trial" (Charlotte, Vermont: Office of Dan Kiley, n.d.).

Undoubtedly, Kiley's greatest wartime accomplishment was his design for the Nuremberg tribunals (figs. 2 and 3). As Chief of the Design Section of the Presentation Branch of the OSS, Kiley was sent to Germany to design the venue for the trial of "Axis criminality." Within five months of arriving in Nuremberg, he had transformed its bombed-out Palace of Justice into the stage for a trial unprecedented in both the nature of its crimes and the international media coverage it received. In addition to providing for representatives of the four Allied victors, Kiley's design accommodated a press corps of several hundred journalists; prepared over 600 rooms for office use; designed the furniture for the courtroom; selected the material for flags, curtains, and seat backs; and (his favorite anecdote) bought the courtroom's carpet on the black market in Paris. For his work, Kiley was honored with the Legion of Merit, conferred by President Truman.

The courtroom arrangement he devised is striking. A typical courtroom configuration would locate the bench at the far end of a rectangular hall facing the adjudicating parties and the audience. Kiley altered the standard arrangement in a simple yet dramatic way. He shifted the international panel of judges ninety degrees to one side, and placed the Nazi defendants facing them. The victims, their representatives, and the world at large were seated, as if in a theater, to witness the trial. A film screen to show Nazi "crimes against humanity" was placed on the wall behind the traditional bench location. This unconventional courtroom design clearly interpreted the subtext of the legal proceedings at hand: justice was served directly to defendants whose crimes were without defense.

With the world at peace, Kiley returned to his civilian practice. Within two years, he was a member of Eero Saarinen's winning team in the competition for the Jefferson National Expansion Memorial in St. Louis, Missouri (fig. 4), the first postwar international design competition. Saarinen, citing competition guidelines that encouraged architects to work with landscape architects, invited Kiley to join his team. His letters to Kiley clearly demonstrate the importance of the landscape architect to the project's concept and success. The jury called their design "a work of genius." In fact the winning entry was almost universally well received.

The Jefferson competition occurred in two phases. The first-phase design, which Kiley preferred, included an upper terrace with garden courts connected by a meandering water course meant to be an abstraction of the Mississippi River. The design is strikingly similar to the 1944 Air Transport Command Passenger Terminal and Operations Building, and reappears in the Cadet Quadrangle Gardens for the 1956 U.S. Air Force Academy. The second-phase design was distinguished by the streamlined, decidedly *moderne* open area, and the asymmetric axial alignment of the arch and the Old Court House beyond.

In the almost two decades that transpired before the project's completion, in utterly altered form, renewed tensions arose between Kiley and National Park Service Director Conrad Wirth about Kiley's landscape plan. This fascinating controversy over Kiley's selection, variety, and quantity of plant materials, and about his modern design intentions (versus those of the more conservative National Park Service), has only recently been explored.[11]

Winning the St. Louis competition certainly brought Kiley international attention, yet he would not be associated with anything comparable, in scale and importance, until the mid-1950s, with his participation in the United States Air Force Academy design. Still, he settled into a varied and active practice that included architecture[12] and landscape architecture as well as planning. While the majority of his work was private, single-family residences, either architecture or landscape or both, it did include a significant complement of diverse projects for governmental, corporate, educational, and religious clients. This work ranged from large master plans (Canadian Aluminum Company of Kitimat, British Columbia, 1951), to interior plantings for small office buildings (James W. Rouse Company Headquarters, Baltimore, 1954), to urban backyards (Society of Friends, Low-Income Housing, Philadelphia, with Oskar Stonorov, Architect, 1953). While today Kiley is often associated only with blue-chip clients, his record throughout the 1950s demonstrates work for clients rich and poor, private and public. In particular, he continued to work with housing developers and government agencies building housing for returning veterans. Also during this period Kiley began making the rounds as a lecturer and critic at American universities and colleges.

11. Regina Bellavia's excellent work on the Jefferson National Expansion Memorial is by far one of the most thorough accounts of Kiley's use and treatment of plant material to affect a desired spatial aim. Using letters, original drawings, and other such primary sources, she delivers an exposition of the "Tulip Tree controversy"—which pitted Kiley against the National Park Service—that yields insights into Kiley's method and design approach, and his specific intentions for the St. Louis project. Further, she provides a detailed picture of complexities involved with large governmental projects, whose protracted and tortuous design and construction techniques can easily defeat even the most experienced practitioner. See Regina M. Bellavia, *Cultural Landscape Report for Jefferson National Expansion Memorial, St. Louis, Missouri* (Omaha, Nebraska: National Park Service, 1996). For Kiley's own perspective on the design, see Bob Moor, "Dan Kiley, Landscape Architect" (St. Louis, Missouri: Oral History Interview, Jefferson National Expansion Memorial, 1994).

12. Kiley is an accomplished architect; in fact, while he never joined the ASLA, he did join the American Institute of Architects. Among his first lectures was one to the Maryland chapter of the AIA in Baltimore in 1953.

Unquestionably the 1950s marked a turning point in Kiley's career; by 1955, with the design of the Miller Garden, the commonly understood canonical Kiley style was fully in place. The critical years leading up to the Miller Garden are the focus of two papers featured here: Daniel Donovan's and Mark Klopfer's essays on Hollin Hills. For Hollin Hills, Kiley designed over ninety gardens between 1953 and 1955; none was ever fully implemented and none survives today in its original state. Not only has Hollin Hills never been discussed as part of Kiley's career, until this decade it has also been virtually ignored.[13] Donovan and Klopfer suggest nothing less than that Hollin Hills was the experimental ground on which Kiley transformed his design language into the masterful modernist idiom for which he is known. It is thus with the Hollin Hills subdivision (a mundane and common site of American landscape practice) and Irwin and Xenia Miller's costly, private residence (the diametric opposite of suburban conformity) that Kiley forged his mature, fully developed style. Henceforth, his designs would be known for their genteel and sophisticated formality, structured by orthogonal geometry and expressed in a vocabulary of forms culled from garden history and the cultured landscape, designs distinguished by an innate sense of proportion and an unerring sense of balance that fit programs to sites in landscapes of extraordinary refinement and clarity.

The Miller Garden is the most representative example of Kiley's mature style. Today it is recognized as Kiley's masterwork, yet this was not so when it was completed. Gary Hilderbrand's contribution to this book underscores the ambivalent attitudes held about the private residential garden in American landscape architectural practice, at least as exhibited by the professional journals of the time. As Hilderbrand notes, the Miller Garden was published in the September 1958 *Architectural Forum* fully three years after it was designed. The article's focus was entirely on Saarinen's house; Kiley's name was mentioned only in a list of the other principals involved. The published landscape plan was truncated and mentioned in a brief caption. The significance of the garden entirely escaped the editors.

The limited exposure Kiley's work received in the article on the Miller Residence was consistent with the treatment of his work by the professional press throughout the 1950s. If his

---

13. Hollin Hills was given a minor acknowledgement in "Planned Outdoor Space," *House and Home* (May 1954): 138–43. Some plans were exhibited at shows at the Architectural League of New York (1996) and at the Architecture Foundation in London (1995).

designs appeared at all, they were most often, if not exclusively, associated with a major architectural project for which he was landscape consultant.[14] When Kiley was mentioned alone, it was, ironically, as architect. Throughout the entire decade, only once was Kiley mentioned in *Landscape Architecture* (October 1951), and that was in relation to a photograph of the low-rent housing project of Middleboro, Massachusetts, on which he had consulted with architects Kennedy and Smith.[15] The same housing development had been featured in the May 1951 *Architectural Record.*

Kiley fared better in trade magazines aimed at individual homeowners and their gardens. *House Beautiful,* under the leadership of Elizabeth Gordon, published Kiley's work as early as 1948, as architect for "the new look" of the American home. In February and November 1951 and again in October 1956, *House Beautiful* featured garden designs by Kiley. Curiously, Joseph E. Howland, who succeeded Gordon as editor of *House Beautiful,* did not include Kiley in his comprehensive 1958 book, *The House Beautiful Book of Gardens and Outdoor Living;* it contained work of Thomas Church, Garret Eckbo, and James Rose, among others, and its cover featured a garden by Innocenti and Webel. When an important book finally published Kiley's work—the Museum of Modern Art's 1964 publication *Modern Gardens and the Landscape,* by Elisabeth B. Kassler—it did not feature the Miller Garden or any of his residential work, but rather the recently completed, monumental modernist landscape he created at the United States Air Force Academy (the Air Garden) and his work for the city of Philadelphia, the Third Block of Independence Mall.

At Colorado Springs, Kiley's initial design for the Cadet Quadrangle Gardens was intended to provide an alternative to the regimentation of cadet life (fig. 5). He created freeform landscaped courtyards, each with a curvilinear walk connecting to adjacent courtyards, thereby offering a continuous strolling course. The loosely configured design contrasted with the orthogonal rigor of the academy's overall scheme. The design resembles those of the Air Transport Command Passenger Terminal and Operations Building and the first phase of the

14. The notable exceptions to the late publication of Dan Kiley's landscape work date to 1941. Margaret O. Goldsmith's *Design for Outdoor Living* (New York: C. W. Stewart, 1941) was the first book to mention Kiley as landscape designer; her book published Kiley's landscape plan for Waverly Oaks, Massachusetts. *The Magazine of Art* (October 1941): 422–7, published an article by Garret Eckbo, "Gardens as Living Space," which included Kiley's "preliminary sketch for the garden of Mr. and Mrs. Kenneth Kassler" and a photo of Kiley's A. A. S. Davy Residence. There is no discussion of Kiley in Eckbo's text, but presumably the Kiley illustrations are meant to reinforce Eckbo's point about contemporary landscape design, "The possibility of integrating architecture and landscape design to produce a broader and more comprehensive art of site-space design" (427).

15. In January 1963 Kiley appeared in *Landscape Architecture* as an author. Dan Kiley, "Nature: The Source of All Design, *Landscape Architecture* (January 1963): 8–10.

Jefferson National Expansion Memorial. Its horticultural variety and abstract complexity differed greatly from what was by mid-1950 supposedly Kiley's characteristic style. The drawings were brought to the final working-drawing stage but were abandoned because of budget constraints.[16] Kiley's inventive and quirky scheme was replaced by an insipid plantation of understory trees and shrubs.[17]

Likewise, Kiley's original concept for Philadelphia's Third Block of Independence Mall reveals a richly textured, architecturally layered design that strongly articulates three-dimensional space through the use of trees and shrubs (fig. 6). Again, the designs were brought to the working-drawing phase but were replaced by a vastly curtailed plan of much less interest. The horticultural variety, so integral to the volumetric concept of the plan, was severely compromised. The sixteen trees and shrubs originally called for were reduced to five; omitted was the majestic cedar of Lebanon (*Cedrus Libani*), which would have provided a striking counterpoint to the geometry of the space.

How ironic that the two landscapes Kassler selected have fared so poorly over time. The United States Air Force actively destroyed Kiley's sublime Air Garden in the mid-1970s, while Philadelphia utilized a more passive, yet proven, means of killing a landscape—neglect.[18] But it might be argued that these projects had been severely compromised prior to their final demise. However contributory to their current state, eleventh-hour design changes to these projects are reminders of the reality of the design process where compromises, imposed changes, and budget and maintenance constraints all factor into the final result. Nonetheless, Kiley's unexecuted drawings (and project correspondence) are revelatory of the richness of his landscape approach. Thus, it is in the unexecuted drawings, not necessarily the realized designs, that we find clues to his creative process.

Dan Kiley's life and career—from modest beginnings in a working-class Boston neighborhood, to enrollment in an Ivy League university, to honor in war, to honor for his art (most recently by President Clinton, who conferred on him the National Medal of Arts), to

---

16. Jory Johnson wrongly states that the Cadet Academic Quadrangle Gardens were never brought beyond preliminary stage. Kiley's drawings indicate otherwise. Kiley's concept was fixed enough for it to be included in the Air Force Academy model built by Skidmore, Owings & Merrill, the architect of the academy. See Jory Johnson, "Man As Nature," in Robert Bruegmann, ed., *Modernism at Mid-Century: The Architecture of the United States Air Force Academy* (Chicago: University of Chicago Press, 1994), 102–20.

17. Kiley's office preserves a rich and important record of the conflicts and problems he faced in the design of the Air Force Academy. By early 1958 Kiley's plans for the Air and Quadrangle gardens were in jeopardy. In a letter to Kiley dated 21 March 1958, Walter Netsch, Jr. of SOM wrote, "it will be impossible to win both quadrangle and the air gardens." In the end the Air Gardens won out. If that were not enough, Air Force authorities challenged at least once Kiley's professional qualifications. See correspondence in the U.S. Air Force Academy project file (Charlotte, Vermont: Office of Dan Kiley, 1950s).

18. Philadelphia's Independence Mall is currently undergoing a total redesign by the firm The Olin Partnership.

professional recognition and achievement that boarders on legendary fame—add to more than just a personal biography—they are nothing short of a major chapter in the history of twentieth-century American landscape architecture. They, along with the corpus of Kiley's work—both drawn and built—only await some enterprising scholar to study, analyze, and put into proper form their history and their story, and thus do justice to the life and work of Daniel Urban Kiley.

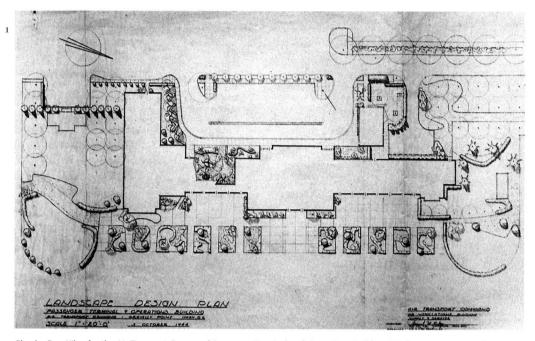

LANDSCAPE DESIGN PLAN

Plan by Dan Kiley for the Air Transport Command Passenger Terminal and Operations Building, Washington, D.C., October 1944 (courtesy Office of Dan Kiley)

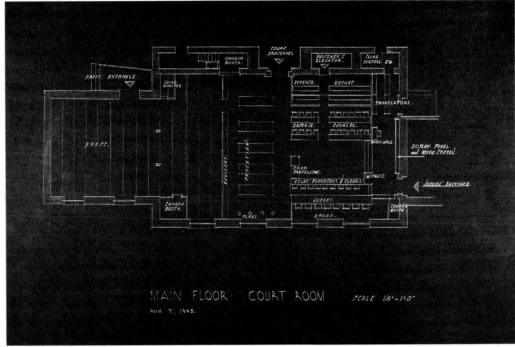

Plan of courtroom design by Kiley for Nuremberg tribunal, November 1945 (courtesy Office of Dan Kiley)

Interior of Kiley's Nuremberg courtroom in mock session, November 1945 (courtesy Office of Dan Kiley)

4

Jefferson National Expansion Memorial Competition, St. Louis, Missouri, 1947 (courtesy Jefferson National Expansion Memorial, National Park Service, St. Louis, Missouri)

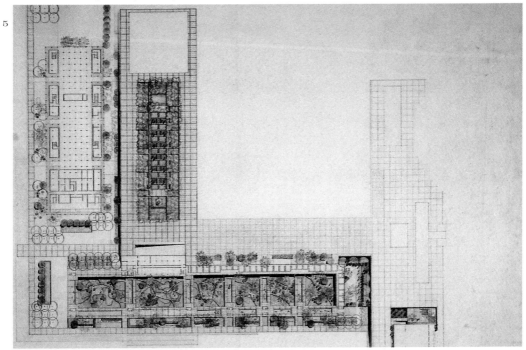

5

Air Gardens and Cadet Quadrangle Gardens, United States Air Force Academy, Colorado Springs, Colorado, c. early 1958 (courtesy Office of Dan Kiley, Frances Loeb Library, Harvard University Graduate School of Design [hereafter FLL])

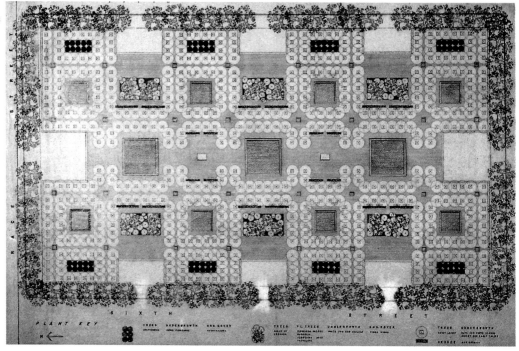

## 6

Third Block of Independence Mall, Philadelphia, Pennsylvania, c. 1960 (FLL)

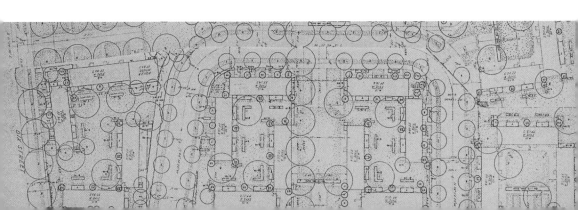

# EARLY HOUSING PROJECTS AND
# GARDEN PROTOTYPES, 1941–52

Anita Berrizbeitia

The main focus of Dan Kiley's work during the early years of his practice was housing, garden prototypes, and private gardens, all conceived primarily in terms of function. Drawings of this work show an emphasis on program, on the material aspects of the gardens, and on the importance given to their ease of maintenance. Displacing the purely aesthetic in favor of the functional allowed Kiley to intervene in areas previously outside the domain of landscape architecture, and thereby to redefine its status within society, effectively expanding its range to address a growing mass culture.

Changes in the conceptualization of objects (both their roles in society as well as their appearance) emerge as reactions against the status quo. New and more adequate artistic practices arise from a critique of those institutions that were providing the social base for those practices.[1] In the language of modernism, this is called the practice of negation.[2] Kiley's early involvement in a practice of negation as a student at the Harvard Graduate School of Design is well known. With fellow classmates Garret Eckbo and James Rose he openly challenged the faculty and the Beaux-Arts curriculum.[3] But his negation was not just protest: it involved a practice that deliberately produced ruptures through the construction of new forms and new relationships between his work and emerging social structures.

Kiley, Eckbo, and Rose were given the opportunity to state their reaction against the landscape architectural establishment in public when they were invited by James Marston Fitch, editor of *Architectural Record*, to write an article on the current state of landscape architecture. The result was the tripartite essays titled "Landscape Design in the Urban Environment" (May 1939, fig. 7), "Landscape Design in the Rural Environment" (August 1939), and "Landscape Design in the Primeval Environment" (February 1940). Before these, the only major treatise on the modern landscape was Christopher Tunnard's *Gardens in the Modern Landscape*, published in 1938.[4] Kiley, Eckbo, and Rose were very familiar with Tunnard's text and it was on the basis of his writings that they had asked Dean Hudnut at Harvard to invite him to teach, which he did from 1939–43.[5] Although there are many connections and similarities between the publications, Kiley, Eckbo, and Rose's approach was very different from

1. T. J. Clark, "More on the Differences between Comrade Greenberg and Ourselves," in Benjamin H. D. Buchloh, Serge Guibault, and David Solkin, eds., *Modernism and Modernity* (Halifax: University of Nova Scotia Press, 1983), 169–87.
2. Ibid., 184.
3. Interview with Dan Kiley, Charlotte, Vermont, 22 August 1997.
4. Christopher Tunnard, *Gardens in the Modern Landscape* (London: Architectural Press, 1938).
5. Interview with Kiley.

Tunnard's. Whereas Tunnard hinged his description of the modern garden on the formal aspects of modern architecture and art, that is, on its aesthetic qualities, Kiley, Eckbo, and Rose explicated the landscape entirely in terms of production in a society structured by industrial capitalism, and specifically of production in the American landscape.

The urban environment, the rural environment, and the primeval environment, referred to in the titles of the articles, are classified according to their predominant mode of production: the urban environment is the result of industry, the rural environment of agriculture, and the primeval, only superficially exploited, of the less intensive activities of trapping and lumbering. Rather than gardens, mass recreation, itself a distinctly modern experience and a product of industrialization, was their focus. Kiley, Eckbo, and Rose discussed mass recreation in terms of production and classified it according to the different functions it had in each productive category. For example, the rural landscape, which has intense cycles of work during the warm months, required enclosed recreation facilities for use primarily during the winter. Distinct from these were urban recreation facilities; because production in the city takes place mostly indoors, recreation was proposed primarily as an outdoor activity, emphasizing fresh air, light, and plant life. Kiley, Eckbo, and Rose also explained recreation types in terms specific to the social environment—for instance, proposing for the rural environment sites such as the bingo hall that promote gatherings and socialization, as a response to the typical isolated working conditions of the farmer.

Within each category—urban, rural, primeval—Kiley, Eckbo, and Rose proposed a classification of recreation types. Unlike nineteenth-century recreation, typically discussed in visual terms, none of these types were described aesthetically, but only according to use, age group, and frequency of distribution in the environment. Thus, for the urban environment they proposed recreation types at many scales, from play lots, children's playgrounds, and district playfields, to urban parks, country parks, and green belts. They also included urban infrastructure such as parkways and freeways, and special areas such as beaches and swimming pools. Rural types of recreation included crafts and visual arts, recreational music (popular orchestras, outdoor concerts, etc.), recreational drama, sports and athletics, and other activities and special events such as field days, community nights, agricultural fairs, and traveling circuses. Recreation in the primeval environment was classified in four types according to intensity of use. Developed recreation, the most intensive, included camping, summer and winter sports, recreational drama, and arts and crafts. Scientific recreation was proposed for special zoological, botanical, and geological areas developed as natural museums. Modified recreation occurred in areas that were modified with the needs of the native population in mind, such as areas for nature tours. Finally, primitive recreation took place in unexplored or partially explored areas and was proposed as an activity in support of the scientific investigation, study, and collection of natural species; it was intended to provide for the "last degree of subjective and emotional need for contact with the primitive."[6]

Thus, each landscape type, rather than being explained in terms of aesthetics, responded to specific functional needs. This was most clearly stated in the urban article: "The approach has shifted, as in building, from the grand manner of axes and façades to specific needs and specific forms to express those needs."[7] As a corollary to this, the program of public parks as traditional, passive sites for contemplation was rejected. A photograph of Bryant Park in New York is captioned as "more decorative than useful." This was contrasted with an image of the Bos Park in Amsterdam, then under construction, captioned as "probably the most advanced intown-park design [that] provides a wide variety of facilities."[8]

Perhaps one of the most controversial proposals in the series was for a complete integration of recreation, work, and living. This was at the time a radical idea, since the paradigm for urban recreation was still the Olmstedian park, conceptualized as the city's counterpoint in its aesthetics and in its program. The conceptual and physical integration of recreation with the city entailed a reinterpretation of the park as one more piece in the productive machinery of the city, rather than as a palliative to the evils of urbanization. Thus Kiley, Eckbo, and Rose conceptually realigned the discipline by proposing that landscape experiences be assimilated into everyday practices and thereby rejected the traditional conception of landscape as a special,

6. Dan Kiley, Garret Eckbo, and James Rose, "Landscape Design in the Primeval Environment," *Architectural Record* (February 1940): 79.
7. Dan Kiley, Garret Eckbo, and James Rose, "Landscape Design in the Urban Environment," *Architectural Record* (May 1939): 77.
8. Ibid., 76.

isolated experience within the chaos of the modern metropolis.

But if for Kiley, Eckbo, and Rose landscape were released from aesthetics, its form remained central to their preoccupations. Form in the modern landscape was based on the conscious observation of the materials of its construction, such as plants, their habit, height, hardiness, soil requirements, deciduousness, color, texture, and time of bloom. This objective observation of the material was less a concern for its cultural references,[9] and more driven by the necessity to put the material to its best use, functionally and biologically. This was cogently stated: "To express this complex of inherent quality, it is necessary to separate the individual from the mass, and arrange different types in organic relation to use, circulation, topography, and existing elements in the landscape. The techniques are more complicated than in the Beaux-Arts patterns, but we thereby achieve volumes of organized space in which people live and play, rather than stand and look."[10] Perhaps no other sentence in the series explains more eloquently the fundamental shift from the purely aesthetic to the functional in the conception of a modern landscape.

What were the sources for the ideas and images in these articles? Christopher Tunnard and Lewis Mumford are quoted in the articles, as well as experts from the United States Department of Agriculture, Works Progress Administration, and Forest Service, to name a few. For their images, which are as telling as the text, they went to the Tennessee Valley Authority, the Farm Security Administration, and the Works Progress Administration, as well as various parks departments (city, state, and federal), the United States Housing Authority (where Eckbo had worked and where Kiley was working at the time), and companies involved in industrial production (such as the Union Pacific Railroad, the Southern Cypress Manufacturers Association, and the Santa Fe Railroad). In other words, they went to those institutions that had built, during the Roosevelt administration, numerous public landscapes— for recreation, transportation, conservation, and production—that embraced mass technology and standardization. They thus forged a conception of landscape that was inseparable from the ideas and processes of industrial production.

9. As in, for instance, the work of Gertrude Jekyll, Jens Jensen, and other regionalists.
10. Kiley, Eckbo, and Rose, "Landscape Design in Urban Environment," 77.

To conclude, one can summarize the three articles as follows: they are a negation of Beaux-Arts principles of design, particularly its principle of structuring space around axes, which renders it inflexible and inorganic. They are a negation of the purely aesthetic and compositional as a basis for design, and of contemplation as a basis for interaction between the landscape and the perceiving subject. Ultimately, they are a negation of the landscape as transcendental and auratic object. Instead, Kiley, Eckbo, and Rose embraced those cultural and economic forces that had to date remained outside the sphere of the discipline: they embraced industrialization, and the accompanying forces of mechanization and rationalization of the everyday, and proposed these forces as the raw material for the development of a new landscape.

The ideas that originated in these articles were realized in the work of the first decade of Kiley's practice, when he was engaged in the design of emerging landscape types: low-budget housing projects for a country that was preparing for war, private gardens for an expanding middle class settling down in the new suburbs, and garden prototypes to be reproduced. While researching for the articles, Kiley was working at the United States Housing Authority in Washington D.C. as "associate town planning architect."[11] He was twenty-seven years old. The Washington years, 1939–41, were crucial for Kiley since it was during this time that he met colleagues with whom he would collaborate during most of his career. Two of the most important friendships he made were with Paul Unger and Louis Kahn. Kiley met Unger at the WPA in 1940 while doing research for the primeval article. He introduced Kiley to the cosmopolitan social life of Washington, where he would meet many of his future clients. That same year Kiley met Louis Kahn on the steps of the Interiors Building. Kahn invited Kiley to work on numerous housing projects with his firm Howe, Stonorov and Kahn. Also through Kahn, Kiley met Eero Saarinen. Through Kahn and Saarinen, Kiley found stimulating collaborative work, and comradeship.

At the United States Housing Authority, Kiley worked on the planning and site design for low-income housing projects. Although this was his first opportunity to try out new ideas, Kiley's boss Elbert Peets did not share Kiley's agenda and found his designs too nonconformist. Likewise, Kiley did not agree with Peets's approach. During the summer of 1941, Kiley left the

---

11. In 1938 Kiley left Harvard and took a job at the National Park Service in Concord, New Hampshire. A few months later he transferred to the Concord Planning Commission to work on the Concord Master Plan. In March 1939, he was offered a job as assistant landscape architect at the Procurement Division, Public Buildings Branch at the Treasury Department and moved to Washington D.C. He resigned after three months to transfer to the United States Housing Authority. His title there was "associate town planning architect" a job that had been held by Garret Eckbo two years earlier. I thank Jane Amidon of the Office of Dan Kiley for providing this information.

Housing Authority to design his first major commission, the Collier Garden in Virginia. The Collier job enabled Kiley to open his own firm, which he based in Franconia, New Hampshire, although his projects were primarily in and around Washington, D.C.

Soon after Kiley's departure from the United Sates Housing Authority, Louis Kahn was hired as a consultant there, and it was as a consultant to Kahn that Kiley was able to work on housing projects away from the shadow of Elbert Peets. In 1941 alone he worked on eight housing projects; of these, five were done in collaboration with Louis Kahn, and a sixth one the following year. In total, the Office of Dan Kiley worked on twenty-one housing projects between 1941 and 1952, done in collaboration with several architecture firms such as Beral & Kastner, Kennedy & Smith, Glasser & Gray, and Stonorov. These projects include two in Washington, D.C.: Lily Ponds Houses of 1942 with Howe & Kahn, and Richardson Dwellings of 1952 with Glasser & Gray.

Lily Ponds Houses and Richardson Dwellings, like his other early housing projects, had low construction budgets, a circumstance that Kiley never bemoaned. Instead, he took advantage of this situation to produce landscapes in which the maximum efficiency was attained with the minimum amount of materials, an idea that was central to the three articles and that had a cultural and conceptual base in the operations of industrial capitalism, such as the division of labor and mass production. For each project, Kiley generated a system, rather than a composition, to arrive at the design. This system is a superimposition of three layers of landscape and program. One layer addressed the individual dwelling unit, another addressed the entire site, and a third the social use of the space, as suggested by the program introduced in the project.

For example, in the Richardson Dwellings the first layer, the topography, was visibly regraded to accommodate the buildings and to differentiate that new topography from the existing surrounding one. A second layer comprised of program elements structured the areas immediately outside the buildings (fig. 8). The semiprivate courtyard spaces formed by the buildings were structured through the repetition of units (fig. 9). These units addressed the functions of living in the individual dwelling: for each apartment there was a tenant planting bed (indicated by a "T" in the plan), a hedge, and accommodations for drying clothes. The public areas around the front of the building were left as open lawns, with the minimum requirements of path to front door and sunken garbage receiver for each unit. Superimposed on the topography and the program was a vegetation layer that addressed the site at a larger scale, particularly with regards to sun orientation and to different scales of streets. The largest trees specified, sycamore (*Platanus orientalis*) and tulip tree (*Liriodendron tulipifera*), are sited to block the hot sun from the south and west. The smaller species, shad (*Amelanchier laevis*), crabapple (*Malus sp.*), hawthorn (*Crataegus sp.*), and redbud (*Cercis canadensis*), articulated the smaller private spaces, closer to the building, as well as the sidewalks that did not require much protection from the sun. Large canopy trees were also used in the interior courtyards to provide shade for seating. While each unit was treated individually, the tree layer unified the property and tied its landscape to the larger environment.

We can also see differentiation of landscape layers in terms of their function at Lily Ponds Houses, a war housing project comprised of 475 dwelling units of cinder block hollow tile and frame on a thirty-acre site (fig. 10). The program for each dwelling unit was identical and included a pea gravel terrace, hedges, and trees for shade (fig. 11). The terraces extended the living areas to the outdoors, and the hedges provided privacy between the units. However, although the terraces and hedges are an extension of the architectural program, they do not reiterate the shape of the building, and therefore stress the landscape's formal autonomy from the architecture in another anti-Beaux-Arts gesture. The tree layer, like that at Richardson Dwellings, was the result of larger-scale environmental and programmatic criteria, such as sun orientation and scale of roads. Large canopy trees line the wide public streets; smaller ones structure the more domestic spaces.

But how can one position such relentless pragmatism and rationality within the discipline of landscape architecture, especially when well-entrenched traditions privilege composition and representation as a basis for design and for achieving signification? One of the fundamental aspects of modern design is the pursuit of the necessary, a process of distillation that eliminates the superfluous in the work by testing it against its own inherent logic. This principle of "fittingness to the material"[12] was reinterpreted through the notion of the division of

---

12. Theodor Adorno, "Functionalism Today" (1965) reprinted in *Oppositions* 17 (Summer 1979): 31.

labor, "understood in its widest sense to include the division of production, the differentiation of work processes and specialization."[13] The breaking up of an activity or operation into tasks in order to produce (and reproduce) objects efficiently entails assigning each material to its most appropriate job. Specialization of materials is evident in the Kiley projects, where all of the elements in the site plans—large canopy trees that shelter from sun and wind, spaces for play, planting beds for the cultivation of food and flowers, and terraces that extend the interior spaces to the outside—carry out objectively prescribed tasks that enable the human use of the site. These elements are arranged on the site according to strictly pragmatic criteria, and not according to compositional devices.

For example, traditional types of planted forms, such as allées, bosques, and groves, that through their various spatial configurations and representational content usually render a landscape with certain aesthetic qualities or values are missing.[14] Instead, plant material is laid out according to the irreducible logic of orientation, soil types, widths of street, and climate control. In other words, the landscape elements are nothing other than means to achieve specific programmatic ends. The conception of landscape as instrument objectifies it as material and strips it of subjective or aesthetic value. Meaning here is, thus, not to be found in the landscape's visual and representational qualities but in the congruence between the material properties of the elements used and their intended functions. To the extent that he was able to succeed, Kiley captured the potential for meaning to exist in the expression of this union.

Like the kinds of landscapes Kiley, Eckbo, and Rose describe as paradigmatic in their articles, the early projects of Kiley transcribe social program and functional necessities into form. Both the articles and the work suggest that meaning in landscape does not reside entirely in the reflection of an autonomous artistic subjectivity, but on the congruence between the systems used to conceptualize and build projects and existing standards of production in society at large.

The idea that design is a set of rational operations that can be reproduced was elaborated in Kiley's early proposals for garden prototypes. In these projects Kiley experimented with a concept rarely explored in landscape architecture: the potential reproducibility of a landscape, when it is conceptualized as standardized program and materials, and not as a

---

13. Georg Simmel, "The Division of Labour as the Cause of the Divergence of Subjective and Objective Culture" (1900), in *The Philosophy of Money*, trans. Tom Bottomore and David Frisby (London: Routledge & Kegan Paul, 1978), 457.

14. In his later work, Kiley reintroduces bosques and allées in his designs, combining these more traditional plant typologies with a modern spatial sensibility. See Greg Bleam, "Modern and Classical Themes in the Work of Dan Kiley," in Marc Treib, ed., *Modern Landscape Architecture: A Critical Review* (Cambridge, Mass: MIT Press, 1993), 220–39.

unique art object. Kiley took on the subject of mass culture and tried to address it through submitting his designs to popular design magazines, such as *Living for Young Homemakers* and *McCall's*. In order to engage a vast and undifferentiated group of people, he presented these landscapes in terms of how they could be occupied, rather than in terms of how they appeared. Techniques, maintenance, and the expression of community (and not the individual subject) were the basis for the design of these prototypes.

For example, Kassler Prototype Garden 1 in Princeton, New Jersey (1950, fig. 12) can be described as an assemblage of materials, vegetal and constructed, that weave together indoor and outdoor space. Kiley understood and articulated this project in terms of technique, labeling the plan as a series of materials, a departure from the traditional way of labeling plans as a series of spaces. Thus, "small ornamental trees," "hedges," "shrub barriers," "screens," "flowers," "raised beds," "shade trees," "paving," "water," "gravel," "sculpture," "stepping stones," and "header boards" replace "bowling green," "overlook lawn," or "terrace-lawn-vista" typically found in formalist gardens. This shows not only Kiley's commitment to expressing landscape in term of its material properties, but also his rejection of a passive, visual engagement of the viewer with the landscape, as inferred in the words "overlook" and "vista" normally present in traditional garden plans. The pragmatism of this design makes the garden seem immune to the subjective will of an artistic personality, further emphasizing its generic and prototypical quality, and its function. This seeming lack of authorship gives the garden the characteristics of a potentially reproducible landscape, one that would be available to society at large.

Kiley's submissions to *McCall's* (1948) and *Living for Young Homemakers* (1951) also investigate standardized garden types but at a larger project scale (six to eight single-family housing units). Again, these gardens were conceived in pragmatic terms of materials, program, and, especially in the *McCall's* proposal, maintenance. Here Kiley addressed a collective culture not only through the unapologetic repetition of elements in each garden, but through siting program elements to promote social exchange between neighbors. For instance, in the *Living for Young Homemakers* proposal (figs. 13 and 14), hedges, pyramidal trees, or screens covered with vines were sited along every other property line (instead of at every property line as in typical plans) to create a semiprivate open lawn, approximately 120 by 60 feet, that was to be shared by contiguous neighbors for lawn games. Similarly, in the *McCall's* proposals, done in collaboration with architect Oscar Stonorov, the individual lawns are delimited by walkways that seem to serve both the individual unit and the entire group (fig. 15). Community in both of these projects was expressed through the landscape's larger organization.

Kiley's interest in standardization is based on his understanding of nature as a process of selection that eliminates the superfluous in order to evolve towards increasing perfection.[15] Kiley explains the difference between what he calls "nature copying"[16] and good design as the difference between looking at the end result of a process and looking at *how* the result got there. This functional study and interpretation of nature allowed Kiley to focus more on material and less on aestheticized aspects of landscape in order to strip it of what were then irrelevant stylistic and representational conventions, and to address emerging social needs.

What is compelling about the early years of Dan Kiley's practice is that they offer an interpretation of the conditions of his times. Inscribed in these projects are a vision of basic human needs—light, air, physical well being, open space, and ease of access to it—that were made available to society at large because of new techniques and artistic inventions in the medium of landscape architecture. It is in the representation of this vision that these projects manifest their meaning. As Kiley himself has said, "Functionalism is everything. It is how you live. It is need. The more visibly a need is expressed in design, the more poetic, because it is real."[17] In his later work, in the so-called blue-chip projects that began with the Miller Garden in 1955, the social agenda present in the housing projects seems to have been replaced by questions of form that focused on more traditional issues of representation and spatiality in gardens. Indeed, it is for his gardens as works of art that Kiley is usually appreciated. His early work, though, redirects our attention beyond questions of style and of the individual designer, and towards those processes that generate the conditions of modern life. The value of this work resides in that it is, ultimately, an effort to reassess the boundaries of the profession in the context of great social and cultural changes, and its potential new roles within the community, the city, and the region.

15. Interview with Kiley
16. Ibid.
17. Ibid.

# LANDSCAPE DESIGN

**by GARRET ECKBO
DANIEL U. KILEY
JAMES C. ROSE**

ALL ORGANISMS SEEK the natural environment most favorable to the complete development of their species, and where nature fails to meet the biologic necessities, adaptation of either environment or organism must occur for life to continue. Each species produces its own forms which provide for its specific requirements in the struggle for existence. In lower organisms, the process of adaptation is so intimately related to the life cycle that it is hardly distinguishable; in vigorously motile and highly socialized organisms, the central forms are no longer individual, but are produced by the community to provide a wider adaptation to satisfy specific needs. The honeycomb of the bees and the beavers' dam are very advanced examples of such forms. Unlike the insects, however, the environmental adaptation of man is infinitely complicated by his own half-social, half-individual makeup, his uneven evolutionary development, and his distribution over every variety of geographic, topographic, and climatic conditions.

Generally speaking, man's central effort—the exploitation of all mineral, plant, animal, and insect forms for his own social welfare—has taken two forms, industrial and agricultural production. Where one of these production forms predominated, a characteristic type of environment resulted—*urban* for industry, *rural* for agriculture, *primeval* for those areas either untouched or only superficially exploited (trapping, lumbering, etc.). Although none of these environments were as socially desirable, efficient, or expressive as they might have been, they served one purpose admirably: they enormously increased man's productivity and laid the material basis for still higher forms of environment.

But as productivity rose, necessary labor time decreased: time for play as well as work became a reality for the average man. This, in turn, posed a new problem: the *absolute necessity* for and the *real possibility* of man's controlling his environment for his pleasure as well as his labor, for recreation as well as production.

WITH INCREASING SHARPNESS, MODERN LIFE POSES the questions: How can man most constructively use his free time? What physical accommodations are essential to his recreation? Who will design them? . . . Since nature—plant life, landscape, open air—are of at least as much importance in this phase of environmental control as architecture, ARCHITECTURAL RECORD has asked Messrs. Eckbo, Kiley, and Rose to explore the subject from the standpoint of landscape design. This study covers recreation in the urban environment; subsequent installments will analyze the rural and primeval.

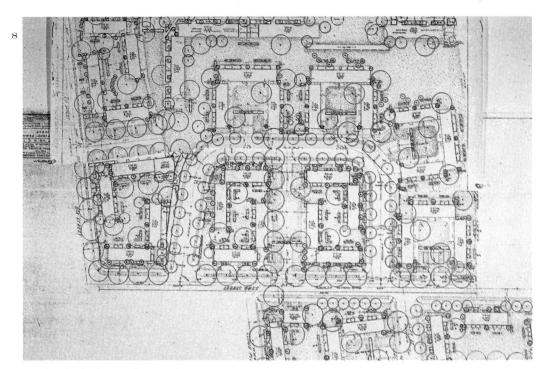

Site plan of Richardson Dwellings, Washington, D.C., 1952 (FLL)

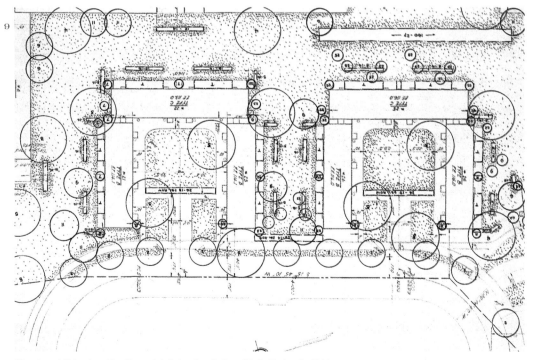

Site plan of Richardson Dwellings, detail showing design of individual units (FLL)

10

Site plan of Lily Ponds Housing, Washington, D.C.,1942 (FLL)

11

Site plan of Lily Ponds Housing, detail showing repetition and serialization in the planting proposal (FLL)

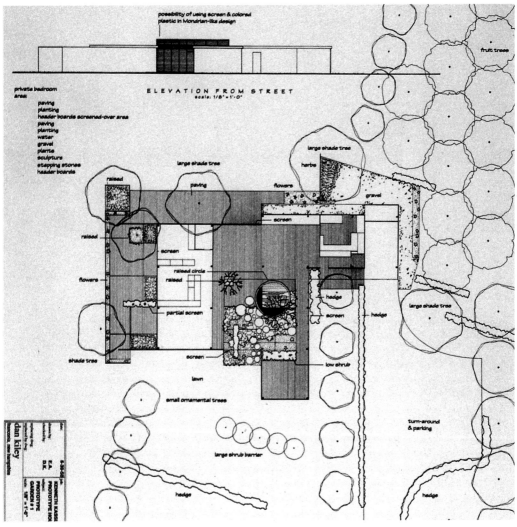

possibility of using screen & colored
plastic in Mondrian-like design

ELEVATION FROM STREET
scale: 1/8" = 1'-0"

private bedroom
area:
  paving
  planting
  header boards screened-over area
  paving
  planting
  water
  gravel
  plants
  sculpture
  stepping stones
  header boards

large shade tree

large shade tree

herbs

raised

paving

flowers

gravel

raised

screen

screen

raised circle

flowers

raised

hedge

partial screen

screen

hedge

shade tree

screen

low shrub

lawn

small ornamental trees

large shade tree

turn-around
& parking

dan kiley

large shrub barrier

hedge

hedge

Detail of plan of Kassler Prototype Garden 1, 1950 (traced from the original reversed sepia by Raphael Justewicz, 1997)

Perspective view of submission for *Living for Young Homemakers Magazine*, 1951 (FLL)

14

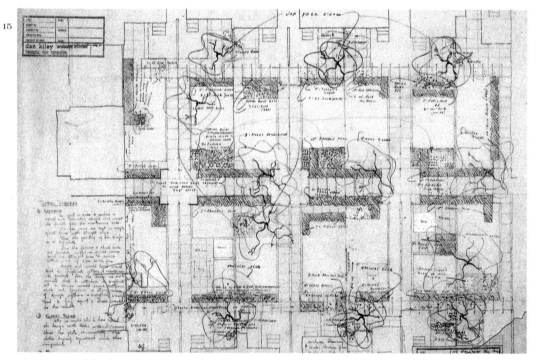

Plan of submission for *Living for Young Homemakers Magazine*, 1951, detail showing individual unit design (FLL)

15

Site plan of submission for *McCall's Magazine*, in collaboration with Oscar Stonorov, architect, 1948 (FLL)

# THE HUNDRED GARDENS

The Social, Historical, and Design Contexts of Hollin Hills

Daniel Donovan

Hollin Hills is a subdivision of 463 houses in Fairfax County, Virginia, south of Washington, D.C., developed beginning in the late 1940s and completed over the next two decades. Robert Davenport, the developer of Hollin Hills, provided landscape designs for homebuyers, who were required to purchase the plans. Dan Kiley was the second of Hollin Hills' three landscape architects, and between 1953 and 1955 he designed gardens for at least ninety-one residences, nearly all of them contiguous, in the section now called Old Hollin Hills.[1]

When I first began researching Hollin Hills, the prospect of uncovering "the hundred gardens"[2] was irresistible. It was soon clear, however, that while Davenport had required that homeowners purchase the landscape design service, installation and plant materials did not go with the plans. Many of the first residents of Hollin Hills—"Hollin Hillers," they call themselves—were transplanted urbanites, veterans drawn to postwar Washington, D.C. jobs, unprepared to face the raw land around their new houses. "We were young and didn't have the money," an original homebuyer said, "and now that we're old, we don't have the energy."[3] (Amateur gardeners were grateful for Davenport's yearly Christmas gift of azaleas to fill their yards.) As far as I have been able to determine, none of Kiley's gardens was installed in its entirety and maintained to the present day. Some plans were followed in part, several extensively (figs. 16 and 17). Only vestiges of a few gardens remain today, in patios, retaining walls, mature trees, and the long-overgrown edges of vegetable plots. Some of Kiley's plant selections did not live, while his vegetable gardens would not grow in the shade. Over the past fifty years, land that might have been gardens on the small lots has been gobbled up by additions—second and third baths, family rooms, double carports and big kitchens—often doubling the size of the original small houses. Hollin Hills and its gardens can nonetheless be considered in three areas of significance: as an intention for a community landscape, as modern design in the mass market, and as a pivotal point in Dan Kiley's career.

Having grown up in Fairfax County in the early 1960s, I recall Hollin Hills as an exotic place where children called their parents by their first names. These people lived in glass houses, drank wine, and read the *New Yorker*. They drove foreign cars. In segregated Virginia,

This essay is based on "Before the Miller Garden: Dan Kiley's Work to 1955," a course offered by the Department of Landscape Architecture at the Harvard University Graduate School of Design in Spring 1997. The seminar examined Kiley's postwar output through the 1950s, and produced case studies of some of the Hollin Hills gardens, along with drawings and models of the properties as designed.

1. While the Kiley archive at the Frances Loeb Library of Harvard's Graduate School of Design contains drawings by Kiley for ninety-five Hollin Hills lots, three of the drawings are not garden designs and one garden design appears to be for a site not actually in Hollin Hills. A checklist of Hollin Hills drawings shown at Harvard's exhibition, Dan Kiley: The First Two Decades, is included at the end of this book.

2. Kiley's name for his work in Hollin Hills.

3. Interviews with Hollin Hills residents, 1996–7.

Hollin Hills was an enclave of social and political liberals, and remains one today. Restrictions on race and religion, common in American housing through most of this century, were from the beginning neither imposed on buyers nor sought by residents. "You are crazy for integration, but you don't know any negroes [*sic*] except for your maid," ran a 1958 description of the stereotypical Hollin Hiller.[4] Some of the first residents formed a neighborhood committee charged with recruiting African-American homebuyers. One former member said, however, "They didn't want these houses—they wanted houses like everyone else's!"[5] Despite the community's overwhelming liberalism, an early covenant remains in force, mandating that proposed house additions and other structures are reviewed by an architectural review committee. The covenant became increasingly contentious as houses changed hands and new residents wanted the garages and big kitchens of "normal" American houses. Residents have left Hollin Hills because of the architectural review committee's decisions, and disagreement over the covenant and the committee continues even today.[6]

Hollin Hills home buyers were among the well-read, museum-going consumers of modern design cultivated by postwar magazines, furnishing and housewares manufacturers, department stores, and cultural institutions. The Museum of Modern Art's "Good Design" series of shows traveled around the country, and through titles like Katherine Morrow Ford and Thomas H. Creighton's *The American House Today* (1951) and John Hancock Callender's *Before You Buy a House* (1953),[7] both of which featured Hollin Hills, a middle-class American could become a connoisseur of design in quality goods from spoons to buildings. Living what Mark Jarzombek called "good-life modernism,"[8] postwar suburbanites came to regard the family home as a showcase for well-chosen, up-to-date furnishings and accessories, and the house itself as a consumer choice. It was in marketing modern design to middle-class consumers in postwar American suburbs such as Hollin Hills that the Bauhaus ideal of artistry in mass production may have come closest to realization.

Hollin Hills was developed at a time when the term "builder's architect" was not pejorative. The problem of mass housing was at the core of the Bauhaus-based curricula

---

4. Hollin Hills Community Association, "-U and Non-U Hollin Hills," *10 Years of Hollin Hills* (c. 1958; reprinted 1989), n.p.

5. Interview with Frank and Anna McKenna, Hollin Hills, 1996.

6. Interviews with Hollin Hills residents.

7. Katherine Morrow Ford and Thomas H. Creighton, *The American House Today* (New York: Reinhold, 1951) and John Hancock Callender, *Before You Buy a House* (New York: Crown Publishers, 1953).

8. Mark Jarzombek, " 'Good-Life Modernism' and Beyond: The American House in the 1950s and 60s: A Commentary," *Cornell Journal of Architecture* 4 (Fall 1990): 76–93.

introduced in American schools of architecture beginning in the 1930s. "Social conscience"—often reinforced by students' experimentation with Depression-era socialism—was believed to be part of an architect's responsibility. Dan Kiley, Garret Eckbo, and other designers trained at Harvard in the late 1930s went on in the next two decades to design migrants' and defense workers' housing, industrialized building systems, and cooperative subdivision tracts. Dan Kiley worked with Lou Kahn on war housing in Washington, D.C., on defense housing at Carver Court in Pennsylvania, and at Ford's wartime city for the bomber plant at Willow Run, planned by Eero Saarinen outside Detroit. At mid-century, the new suburbs were there for landscape architects and architects to design. They became an extension of the profession's responsibility and a natural place to apply the ideals of the time. Even Mies van der Rohe came up with a steel-frame "builder's house" in 1955, meant to sell on the mass market for $15,000.

Like most people in the market for new homes after the war, Hollin Hillers were new to the suburbs. Along with the government, Washington, D.C. had grown dramatically during the Depression and the war. Federal jobs attracted homebuyers (many from northern cities) to the Washington area. More than half of the men in Hollin Hills worked in the middle and upper levels of the federal government. There was little advertising for the development. Publicity came through benefit home tours or features in *Life, Better Homes and Gardens,* and the Washington newspapers. But word of mouth attracted most of the early buyers.[9] Builders and architects learned of Hollin Hills through articles in *Architectural Forum* and *Architectural Record.*[10] Sales brochures promised "American architecture at its best" (fig. 18), avoiding the associations with other times and places that other developments sold. The architecture of Hollin Hills' houses employed none of the American images seen in adjoining developments. Hollin Hills instead offered rational design. The first Hollin Hills models, designed by architect Charles Goodman, were numbered, not named, and a string of letters after the number was code for lower bedrooms, basements opening on grade, an extra module in the kitchen, or other modifications to the model.

9. Interviews with Hollin Hills residents.

10. See "Builder's Project: Combines Intelligent Land-Planning, Handsome House Design, a Unique Merchandising Plan. Result: A Pacesetting Subdivision in the $10,000–$25,000 Price Field," Architectural Forum (December 1949): 80–83 and "Parent's Magazine Announces Winners of Home Competition for 'Best Homes for Family Living,'" Architectural Record (November 1951): 110.

By the time Dan Kiley became involved in 1953, however, the modestly priced family houses offered in Hollin Hills included not only the elegant ranchlike models (the roof of the 1948 model 2 was literally inverted for the 1953 model year, lifting a new V-shape over continuous clerestory windows), but new designs from the mainstream of the modern movement in architecture. One model had the butterfly roof of Marcel Breuer's 1949 Exhibition House for the garden of the Museum of Modern Art. Model 5 interpreted Philip Johnson's Glass House in a wood-frame pavilion that sold for $16,500; in 1954 *House + Home* called it "the most advanced builder's house in America."[11] Although the houses were not prefabricated, Hollin Hills models shared some modular components, and went without ornament in favor of materials, proportion, and structural expression to distinguish the architecture.

Even more radically different than the houses was the design of the land. The Hollin Hills garden owner was also a "householder" in a community landscape, one of many gardeners in an intended larger design (fig. 19). Literally "buying into" a shared landscape of borrowed views and common amenities, the householder's role in the community was much greater than that of homeowners in other subdivisions, where typically only the front yard was on display. The landscape design for Hollin Hills critiqued notions of self and property in a way that was deeply "un-American." Robert Davenport, Charles Goodman, and landscape architect Lou Bernard Voight planned Hollin Hills around community parks, pedestrian paths, and school sites.

Davenport and Goodman began by shaping roads and house sites to the hilly contours of the former farmland, forested with second growth, mostly deciduous trees (fig. 21). In contrast to the usual practice of the day, they did not strip and replant the land, but instead preserved the understory along the backs of the houses, and as many trees as possible everywhere. Not all lots in Old Hollin Hills had driveways (people had fewer cars in the early 1950s), and many residents still leave their cars on the street. Those driveways that were built were not surfaced, and it was the developer's intention for the roads as well, until county officials insisted on them being paved. Even so the roads in Old Hollin Hills have neither sidewalks nor curbs. Streetlights were not planned, and some residents still regret the arrival of lights in the 1960s.

11. "This Utility Core Plan Sells the Most Advanced Builder House in the U.S.," *House + Home* (January 1954): 140–3.

The developer did not add new plantings. Rather the lots were intended to be planted by the homeowner according to plans provided at purchase.

Hollin Hills' landscape designers—especially Lou Bernard Voight and Dan Kiley in Old Hollin Hills, and Eric Paepke there and later in New Hollin Hills—used the gardens to rethink, reinterpret, and deliberately confound American notions of front and back yards. Informality and outdoor living de-emphasized the front door. Many owners, especially those in model 5, have never used what was intended to be the front door. Many houses did without lawns. Play areas, barbecues, and clotheslines (no one could afford a dryer) appeared in front yards (fig. 22).[12] To county officials' further consternation, Hollin Hills' site planners placed houses at odd angles to each other and to the street frontage. Despite small lots, the usual ranks of lined-up houses and parallel property lines were avoided in favor of lots shaped to the land and siting that minimized neighbors' awareness of each other (fig. 20). (Fences have never been allowed.) Plantings emphasized long views at the same time that they screened indoor and outdoor living areas. Shared play lots and plant groupings blurred property lines. People enjoyed a landscape larger than what they owned: while they "borrowed" each other's scenery, they also got a lawn large enough for volleyball. Intriguingly, Dan Kiley let one pair of neighbors share a vegetable garden, cut on the bias by the property line, but he provided no planting plan for it.

Landscape design in Hollin Hills began with Lou Bernard Voight, who had been a student with Dan Kiley at Harvard in the late 1930s. During the war, Voight taught at Black Mountain College in North Carolina, and later worked for Skidmore Owings & Merrill on the planning of Oak Ridge, Tennessee. Following the war, he opened a landscape architecture practice in Bethesda, Maryland. In 1948, on Dan Kiley's recommendation, Voight began his association with the office of Charles Goodman and Associates, planning and designing for Hollin Hills and other Goodman designs. For five years Robert Davenport paid Voight $100 for each garden design. Voight's last gardens for Hollin Hills are dated 1953, the year he died.

At Goodman's request, Kiley immediately took on Voight's role in Hollin Hills, and some of the earliest gardens in Kiley's archive still bear Voight's rubber-stamp title block.

12. Interview with Laura Tenny Brogna, 1997; Brogna, a Harvard Graduate School of Design 1997 landscape graduate, grew up in Hollin Hills in the 1970s in a model 5 that Kiley identifies as the Briggs Residence.

Goodman, a graduate of the Illinois Institute of Technology, was several years Kiley's senior. In 1940, Kiley had opened an office in Washington, D.C., where he was part of a small network of architects designing in the modern style, including Goodman and Edward Durrell Stone. Late in the war, Kiley worked with Goodman on the Air Transport Command Passenger Terminal and Operations Building at Washington's National Airport (1944). Following Hollin Hills, Kiley and Goodman worked together again on the Officers' Club at Andrews Air Force Base near Washington, D.C. in Prince George's County, Maryland (1958).

One of Kiley's first Hollin Hills designs was a landscape for model 5 on Paul Spring Road, the advanced pavilionlike house *House + Home* would praise in 1954.[13] Installed nearly overnight, the garden pictured in black-and-white in *House + Home* and in color in *Better Homes and Gardens*[14] is probably the most complete installation of any of Kiley's designs for Hollin Hills. The magazine photographs and Kiley's drawing show a canted terrace at the end of a flagstone walkway that angles around an existing tree. Close to the house, retaining walls, walks, flower beds, and screens around the drying yard clearly respond to the rectilinear architecture of the house, while planting groups become looser the farther they are from the house. Like nearly all Hollin Hills yards, that here has gone back to woods; only a few mature trees can be recognized from the photographs.

Hollin Hills was a sudden and inconvenient job for Kiley. In 1945, he had moved his office to Charlotte, Vermont, and communication with Virginia was awkward. The modern architects Kiley had known before and during the war had established practices, and through them blue-chip commissions—the Air Force Academy, the Miller Garden, corporate parks, and big houses—began to come into his office. On his first day on the Hollin Hills job, Kiley saw eight clients, six on his second, and four his third. He could not meet everyone; some of the owners simply picked up plans mailed from Charlotte to the sales office. These may be the plans with generic programs, contrasting with the more detailed designs for the people interviewed (fig. 23). The latter highly programmed spaces reveal their owners' dreams—or maybe Vermont winter fantasies: pools and tennis courts, sculpture gardens, darkroom sheds, "children's

13. "This Utility Core."
14. Helen Stark, "An Experiment with Floor Space," *Better Homes and Gardens* (June 1954): 70–1, 164–6ff.

stages," even yard-sized model railroads (fig. 24). Kiley talked Davenport into raising his fee to $150 per garden—he said he "had to pay his draftsman."[15]

Kiley's office continued to design gardens for Hollin Hills through 1955, completing the part of the development known as Old Hollin Hills. On the drawings, the initials "E. P." refer to Eric Paepke, whose drawings are distinguished by cursive lettering (fig. 25)—Paepke's printing was barely legible, Kiley claimed. Paepke left Kiley's office and established his own in Alexandria, Virginia, where until 1971 he designed gardens for the flatter contours of New Hollin Hills.

With little time and one hundred gardens to design, "[I pulled out] all the tricks," Kiley said, "everything that came into my head. If I had a week, I probably would have spoiled them."[16] All of the gardens share a parti in which formal areas "hold the house," as Kiley put it, while more naturalistic plantings sit away from the house (fig. 26). In the larger landscape, shaped as much by Davenport, Goodman, and Voight as by Kiley, the managed views, continuous planting groups, and neighborhood amenities recall socialist ideals of the 1930s and the series of articles Kiley co-authored with Garret Eckbo and James Rose late in those years. Kiley's gardens for small urban lots (fig. 15) published in *McCall's* in 1948, and his 1951 designs for small suburban gardens for *Living for Young Homemakers* magazine,[17] propose shared lawns and game areas, reprogramming front and back yards and blurring the property lines—themes that reappear in Hollin Hills.

"The hundred gardens" were a kind of design laboratory for Kiley's practice, and a shift in his style at the time is apparent. As a student at Harvard Kiley rejected the Beaux-Arts bias of the Department of Landscape Architecture in favor of the modernism Walter Gropius was introducing to the architecture students. In the prewar and early postwar years, Kiley's asymmetrical, free-form modernism, like that of Eckbo, Rose, and Thomas Church, borrowed the angular and biomorphic shapes of cubist and surrealist painting. Kiley credits the radical change in his style in the early 1950s to his first visits to André Le Nôtre's seventeenth-century French gardens in 1945. Kiley's garden of ten years later in Columbus, Indiana, for Irwin and

15. Interview with Dan Kiley, East Farm, Charlotte, Vermont, June 1997.
16. Ibid.
17. The magazine references are taken from titles of drawings in the Kiley archive. The author has not been able to find either article.

Xenia Miller is regarded as the first example of Kiley's so-called neoclassical style ("Forget the 'neo,'" Kiley has said about the garden in Columbus[18]), as well as, by many, the finest American garden in the modern style. The significance of the Miller Garden lies in the way that Kiley took the Beaux-Arts devices against which he had rebelled—axis, symmetry, grid, repetition— and adapted them to a modern sensibility of space, movement, enclosure, and transparency. Kiley's last garden designs for Hollin Hills predate the Miller Garden but show his mature style (fig. 27); this style is also forecast in the garden for the Baker House of 1951 by Minoru Yamasaki (fig. 28) and more than suggested in the garden for the Osborne House of 1954 by Edward Larrabee Barnes (fig. 29). Kiley says that he began work on the Miller Garden in 1953, the year of his first gardens in Hollin Hills.[19] Though these early gardens continue Voight's free-form gestures and shapes (figs. 30 and 31), two years and nearly a hundred gardens later, the highly orthogonal designs for Hollin Hills clearly display the signature allées, bosques, and grids of the Miller Garden, and of Kiley's mature style.

One example of this is the graveled allée of aspens that follows the property line between the Wald and Buffmire houses on Glasgow Road (figs. 32 and 33). Though it would have more likely terminated in a swing set than in a Henry Moore sculpture, the device nonetheless works between the Wald's back lawn and the Buffmire's play yard much as the sidelong axis does so memorably in the Miller Garden: as axis and screen, wall and threshold, by turns opaque and transparent, ordered by and ordering the architecture around it.

Though my students suspected that, had all the hundred gardens been installed, the combination would have been both precious and overwhelming, Hollin Hillers say they like the way their neighborhood has "returned to the woods" in the five decades they have lived there. Indeed the unfenced back yards of Old Hollin Hills share a continuous "natural" understory under indigenous trees, and extensive ivy (unforeseen by Kiley and a creeping plague to many homeowners) has supplanted many front lawns. Even though little remains to suggest the landscape the hundred gardens might have made, a walk in Hollin Hills is still Dan Kiley's "walk in the woods."[20]

---

18. Cited in Warren T. Byrd, Jr., and Reuben Rainey, eds., *The Work of Dan Kiley: A Dialogue on Design Theory* (Charlottesville: University of Virginia, 1983), 10.

19. Interview with Kiley.

20. One of Kiley's favorite metaphors is "I keep saying that landscape architecture should be like a walk in the woods; it should have that sense of mystery and perpetual growth, moving through and going on and on, without stopping." Cited in Brendan Gill, "The Garden Artist," *New Yorker* (16 October 1995): 143.

Today the land in Hollin Hills (fig. 34) is more valuable on the market than any of the few houses remaining in their original condition—1000 square-foot houses with one bathroom are substandard in a market where "general average living requirements" include dryers and security systems, along with great rooms, two-car garages, and master-bath suites. At the same time, Hollin Hills has become a neighborhood of "fabulous 40's homes."[21] Ironically Hollin Hills' modern architecture, intended to transcend style in the 1940s, today attracts a new, much more affluent generation of homebuyers. Plate glass and butterfly roofs are for these consumers very much about style. Most early buyers chose Hollin Hills not only because the architecture was to their taste, but also because they shared an outlook on life they believed the design represented. Dan Kiley's pivotal work for the development contributed to both of these themes.

21. Sara Amy Leach, "Fabulous 40's Homes," *New Dominion: The Magazine for and about Northern Virginia* 1, no. 4 (Fall 1987): 84–6.

# THEME AND VARIATION AT HOLLIN HILLS
A Typological Investigation

Mark A. Klopfer

Daniel Urban Kiley's early work contains a wide spectrum of design strategies, influences, and processes. Viewing his series of residential garden projects for Hollin Hills, Virginia (1953–55) through the lens of typology, however, allows a clearer understanding of both his process leading to the Miller Garden (1955–57) and the design language he has employed and refined since the early 1950s. Though unbuilt, these proposals exhibit both the development of design elements and the grammar with which the elements are combined that became characteristic of Kiley's work.

These design elements were developed under constraints of economy, modest scale, and need for expedient production (as well as Kiley's low $150 commission per project). Individually, none of the projects at Hollin Hills is of special merit, but together they reveal their important role as a design laboratory for Kiley. An examination of these projects, and their elements, is also important as documentation of Kiley's stylistic transformation. As a series of solutions presented for the same design problem, namely the middle-class residential landscape, the projects for Hollin Hills recount Kiley's transition from a modern design language founded in eclectic influences to one of greater abstraction and elemental use of landscape types.

Because commissions at Hollin Hills were tied to when a lot was sold, unifying design strategies on a scale larger than the individual lot, and its adjacent neighbors, were unlikely. Therefore the elements of the individual schemes—plinth, clearing, edge, allée, orchard, and bosque—and the formal rules governing them became the primary objects of investigation at Hollin Hills. These types ultimately reappeared in their fully articulated and refined form in the Miller Garden, which provided a much more generous scale and budget.

Despite the rolling topography of the subdivision, Kiley rarely used it as a design medium. The Barnard (5 May 1953) and Risley (12 August 1953) gardens, both done very early, are exceptions to this. In both, topography is the basis of a geometric plinth—one round, one square—on which both the house and a series of programmed outdoor spaces are sited. This strategy allows for the shift of geometries between the house and the site parcel to become disengaged, so that programmed spaces on the plinth are given order and set in contrast to the irregular and formless residual spaces surrounding them.

More typically, the dramatic slope of the ground is absorbed by the house itself, and earth plinths are created more as site elements than as site strategies. The Hill Garden (12 April 1954, fig. 24) best illustrates this in its use of a wooden bridge to connect the house to the street. The approach from the street allows entry into the top floor of the house, while the level below exits directly at grade to the rear yard. Whimsical elements are found in many of the proposals. Here a children's play slide at midspan connects the bridge to a play area built on a plinth below.

In many schemes spaces are seemingly subtracted out of the woodland to create strong figural clearings. An early series of projects employs the clearing as a type: the primary design strategy is to clear a central space behind the house and often to introduce new vegetation at the edges of the space to provide a screen from the adjacent properties. The Rosen (5 August 1953, fig. 35) and Sorkin gardens (14 October 1953) are the earliest of this type and divide the parcels into a tripartite composition (prefiguring the similar tripartite organization of the Miller Garden). The first part is the vegetation completely surrounding the house. The middle zone is lined with ornamental plantings and is thereby differentiated from the furthest space, which is left vacant and has a less-direct connection with the house.

In a series of gardens done nearly a year later, the clearing as a design type emerges again, only this time more careful attention is paid to the enclosure of the space and its figural delineation. In the first of this series, the Klenk Garden (7 December 1954, fig. 36), a more loosely defined clearing is formed, reinforced by a circumambulating walk that allows access to the entire site. The edge here simulates a natural woodland edge; several existing trees are retained as specimen trees. A similar parti with a circumambulating path is found in the London Garden (12 December 1954). Here, however, what had been the large central space in the Klenk Garden is filled, and an ellipse of lawn, bordered by a stone wall and a ring of azalea shrubs, is subtracted from the mass of the vegetation. The edge adjacent to the figure is made dense with vegetation and topographical change in the form of the wall, so that the open quality of the space is more clearly opposed to that of the woodland. In the Feldman Garden (15 December 1954, fig. 37), this approach is developed on a larger scale and made more complex through the introduction of a line of tulip poplars underplanted with Japanese flowering quince, creating a geometrically ordered edge adjacent to the house, while the remainder of the irregular outline of the space is again defined by a simulated woodland edge.

As seen in the Hollin Hills projects that employ the clearing as their primary type, the creation of discrete, vegetal walls forming edges was an important component of Kiley's evolving design language. In many cases an articulated edge is created at the site boundary, either between sites or along the street, so as to establish a distinct place in which to create the garden. In the Barnard Garden, and in most of the early schemes, the edge created is irregular and blends with the existing woodland vegetation. The development of the edge as a primary element in Kiley's design strategy begins with its articulation as a geometrically ordered object. Three parcels that together act as an entrance to the subdivision on Rebecca Drive show Kiley's growing interest in the possibilities of the edge condition and chronicle the increasing complexity of this typology. The Daugherty Garden (31 July 1953, fig. 38), which sits on the corner of Rebecca Drive and the arterial Paul Spring Road, starts the sequence with a series of seventeen Canadian hemlock trees laid out in a zigzag hedge along Rebecca Road. The adjacent Moore Garden (9 September 1953) continues the hedge but introduces a line of London plane trees running along the street at the rhythm established by the hedge. In the last parcel, the Leighton Garden (24 January 1955, fig. 39), the London plane trees are underlain with Wichura rose, which gives the edge a complex mix of groundcover, understory, and canopy elements.

By August 1954 and the Rogin Garden (fig. 40), Kiley was defining a regularized system for treating the edges of the property and developing a planting palette that he would use throughout the remainder of the Hollin Hills projects and many projects throughout his career. In the rear of the Rogin Garden, the two programmed areas, divided by a freestanding wood screen, are separated from the adjacent lots by green privacy walls. Planes, comprised of Canadian hemlock to the east and red pine to the west, also act as freestanding green walls, asymmetrically placed at the perimeter of the two spaces. The front of the lot is lined with a row of eight tulip poplars behind a privet hedge. The eight trees on the Rogin property form part of a longer line that is staggered as it crosses five lots, forming a consistent street edge. To the rear, a double row of twenty fruit trees is reconfigured from a typical grid to make an edge reinforced on the inside with two lines of English yew.

Kiley's interest in the French garden is in part seen by the use of the allée as a type. In the French garden, the allée functioned as both a promenade and an extension of a view. Typically the allée was terminated with either an element such as a statue or pavilion or was visually extended to an apparently infinite distance at the horizon. At Hollin Hills, the scale of the parcels made the inclusion of all of the traditional elements of the allée impossible. Instead Kiley abstracted the elements and still retained the sense of a promenade in a clearly defined linear space, although this was usually relegated to a driveway or small garden path.

The introduction of the allée came late within the projects for Hollin Hills. The example holding most closely to the type is found in the Wald Garden (2 February 1955, fig. 32). Here an allée of quaking aspen and flanking beds of myrtle and box barberry lines a gravel path. The allée begins adjacent to the house and runs to the rear corner of the lot. Serving no real circulatory purpose, it acts more as a screen from the adjacent Buffmire Garden than as a functional circulation connection between two points. The Buffmire Garden (7 February 1955, fig. 33) itself contains an allée in a greatly reduced form to its western edge. Here a paved walk is flanked on one side with a series of willow oaks, each pair bracketed by an alternating hedge of red pine, a strategy presaging some of the allée elements of the Miller Garden. Projects completed after this important pair of gardens in the Hollin Hills series, such as the Vorhis (27 June 1955, fig. 41) and Kanarek (30 June 1955) gardens, also exhibit qualities of the allée. Here Kiley gives a rhythm to the entry sequence of the driveway, again presaging the entrance drive at the Miller Garden.

In many of the schemes for Hollin Hills, Kiley capitalizes on the disparate qualities of irregular woodland and geometrically designed elements. In particular geometrical plantings of trees have become a hallmark of Kiley landscapes. While examples exist prior to the projects for Hollin Hills, the importance of these elements becomes clearer in these projects. His first design for the Hollin Hills projects was the developer's model house (5 May 1953), whose formally irregular landscape takes its cues from Lou Bernard Voight, whom Kiley succeeded as landscape architect for Hollin Hills. Other early schemes, such as that for the Wayne (7 June 1953, fig. 42) and Record (21 July 1953) gardens, contain elements of geometrical plantings primarily in doubled and staggered lines.

With this design for Mr. and Mrs. Adrienne Spivack (6 August 1953, fig. 43), Kiley transformed what appeared in earlier designs as a row or double row of trees along the street to an orchard of fruit trees. This type is often specifically designated "orchard" by Kiley on the plans and typically is comprised of dwarf fruit trees laid out on a grid. In the Spivack plan, the grid establishes the first layer of an orthogonal layering system that runs from the orchard through the house, and composes several bands of outdoor living spaces to the rear of the house. In the Seeman Garden (23 July 1954), one of the only projects in the Hollin Hills series where the house is placed orthogonal to the site boundaries and street, the grid is present again in the fruit orchard, but has also developed a larger organizing role for the rest of the garden, which is divided into rooms. Separated by hedges and paving, these highly programmed spaces hint at the more elaborate articulation of the same spatial and programmatic strategies as those at the Miller Garden. The orchard, here containing only nine trees and clearly articulated as an object, partially fills the center of the rear yard, and prefigures a similar treatment of the redbud bosques in the Miller Garden's mature garden.

The Wald and Buffmire gardens employ both orchard and bosque types in tandem with other devices, such as hedges and freestanding planes. The bosque type, though not labeled on the projects for Hollin Hills, is described as such on the drawings of the Miller Garden and is mostly comprised of non-fruit trees laid out in a grid. The spacing either permits or denies entry into the bosque, thereby functioning as either garden room or object barrier.

The Buffmire Garden shows the most elaborate use of gridded planting, which occurs in this plan at three scales and with three types of vegetation. An apple orchard planted with eighteen-foot spacing—in concert with layers of Japanese Barberry and Wichura rose—separates the house from the street. In contrast to the open grid of the orchard, a tightly spaced bosque of quaking aspens, spaced only five and a half feet apart, creates a mass that terminates the driveway and reorients the entry sequence. Another bosque exists in the mass of trees just east of the driveway, where red pine is also planted very tightly on a five-foot grid to form a more solid wall than that of the aspens. The Buffmire plan is similar to that of the Miller Garden not only in its employment of the grid, but also in its use of a freestanding plane to separate the service courts to the west of the driveway from the entry sequence. The edge condition of alternating opening and mass, here composed of red pine, is set against the rhythm of seven willow oaks to create privacy along the site's western edge. This strategy is very similar to the alternating arborvitae hedges employed at the edges of the Miller Garden.

The typologies that Kiley initiated in his projects for Hollin Hills continued to develop throughout his career. His abstraction and reduction of these types might be viewed as gestures to larger landscape types: the hill or other geomorphologic landform, cleared space within a forest, understory or transitional edge, path, cultivated grove, and forest. In Kiley's work these are reduced to their most essential and compact forms and employed under a modernist idiom. As a result the typology is used formally, not for its semantic content. However, as Giulio Carlo Argan proposes in his investigation of typology,[1] is it not possible for typology to imbue landscape design with meaning that moves beyond form? To Argan, the value of using types, as defined by Quatremère de Quincy, is that, in their generic form, types avoid the problems of imitation inherent to the use of a specific model or precedent, and therefore allow new interpretation and expression, while still being guided by the idea of an element that should itself serve as a rule for the model. Formally, Kiley's work points a direction that a typology of landscape might take, and—when executed in relation to the technological and cultural forces that shape it—might display a new layer of meaning.

1. Giulio Carlo Argan, "On the Typology of Architecture" (1962); reprinted in *Architectural Design* 33 (December 1963): 564–5, translated by Joseph Rykwert.

Norma Odum on the patio of her home, 1955 (Norman Odum)

Odum Garden, 1955 (Norman Odum)

# "... American Architecture at its best"*

### RECOGNITION

Southwest Research Institute
Certificate of Merit

Parents Magazine
Two Awards, 1952
One Award, 1957

D. C. Chapter, AIA and Evening Star
Awards for Residential Architecture
1955, 1956, 1957
AIA Regional Competition Award, 1956

National AIA Centennial Competition
Two Awards, 1957

Included in AIA exhibit at National Gallery of Art, "10 Milestones in the Future of America's Architecture"

* Quoted from AIA Centennial Booklet, "100 Years of Architecture in America," in which Hollin Hills is featured.

HOLLIN HILLS • 1223 FORT HUNT ROAD • ALEXANDRIA, VA

Brochure cover, c. 1960 (courtesy Alan Warshawer)

Aerial photograph, Hollin Hills, c. 1958 (courtesy Hollin Hills Homeowners Association)

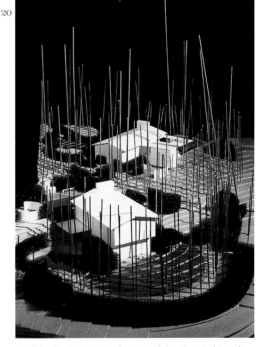

Models of Odum House (foreground, by Chisa Toda) and Coyne House (background, by Shinnichi Kaburagi), 1997

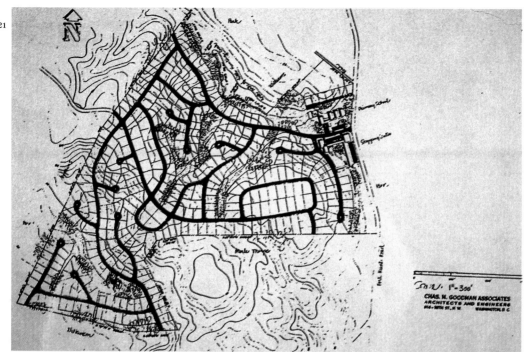

Site plan, Hollin Hills, c. 1950 (courtesy Charles M. Goodman and Associates)

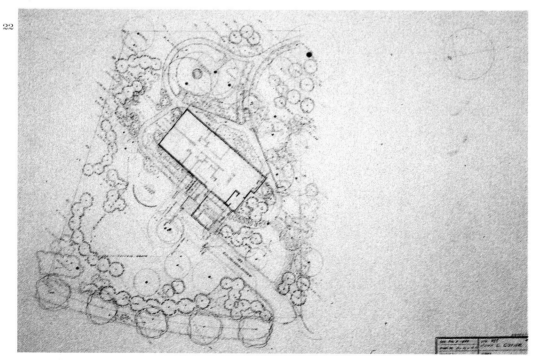

Coyne Garden, 3 August 1953 (FLL)

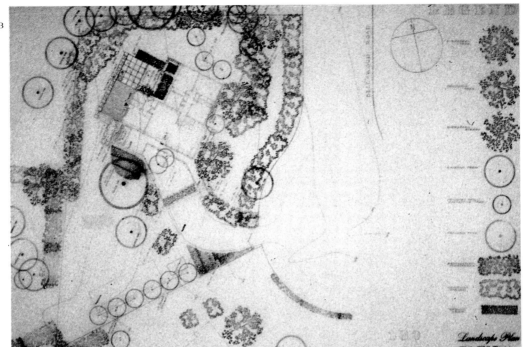

Kenen Garden, 4 February 1954 (FLL)

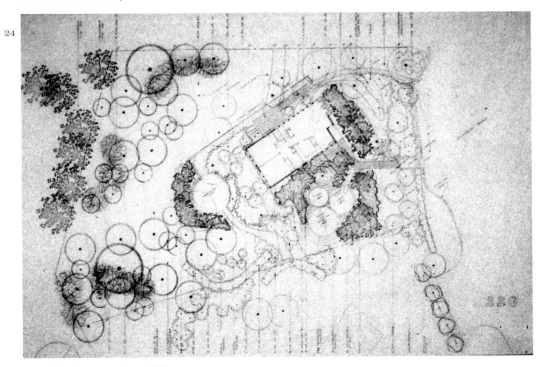

D. P. Hill Garden, 12 April 1954 (FLL)

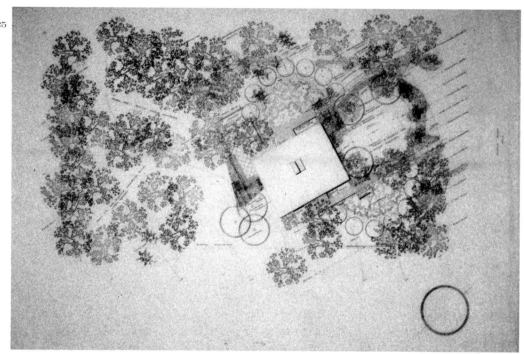

Odoroff Garden, 13 January 1955 (FLL)

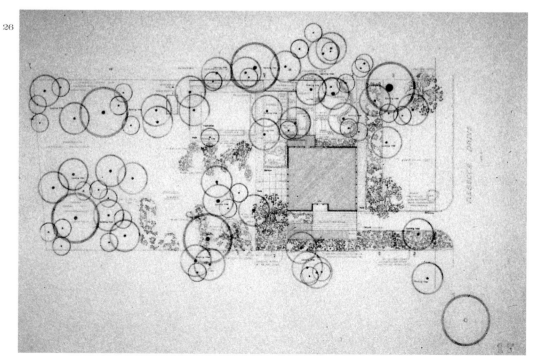

E. F. Preston Garden, 20 June 1955 (FLL)

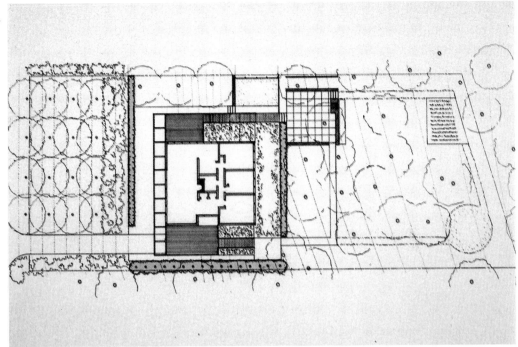

Briggs Garden, 13 May 1955 (redrawn by Laura Tenny Brogna, 1997)

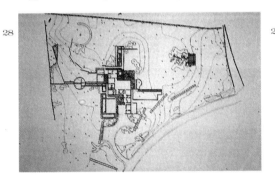

Baker Garden, 1951; house by Minoru Yamasaki (FLL)

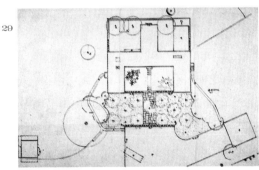

Osborne Garden, 1953; house by Edward Larrabee Barnes (FLL)

Goding Garden, 24 September 1953 (FLL)

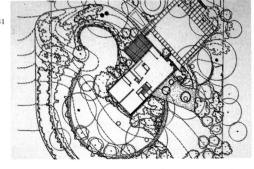

Mr. and Mrs. Raymond E. Odum Garden, 4 August 1953
(redrawn by Chisa Toda, 1997)

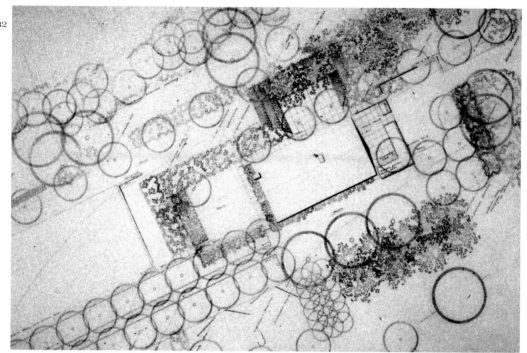

Wald Garden, 2 February 1955 (FLL)

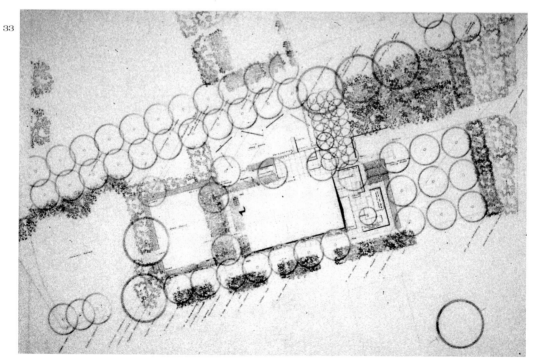

Buffmire Garden, 7 February 1955 (FLL)

34

Hollin Hills street scene, 1997 (Daniel Donovan)

35

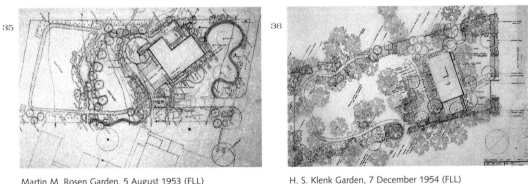

Martin M. Rosen Garden, 5 August 1953 (FLL)

36

H. S. Klenk Garden, 7 December 1954 (FLL)

37

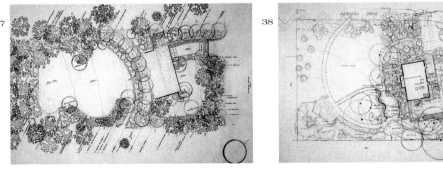

Charles Feldman Garden, 15 December 1954 (FLL)

38

Daugherty Garden, 31 July 1953 (FLL)

R. M. Leighton Garden, 24 January 1954 (FLL)

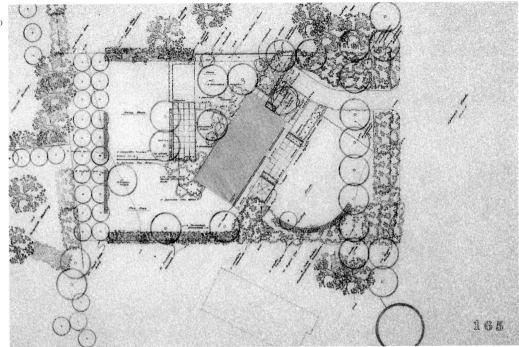

40

165

Martin Rogin Garden, 17 August 1954 (FLL)

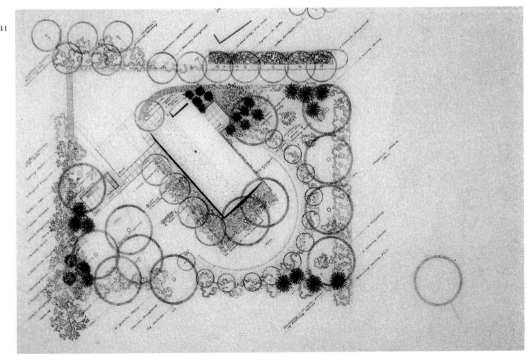

41

D. G. Vorhis Garden, 27 June 1955 (FLL)

42

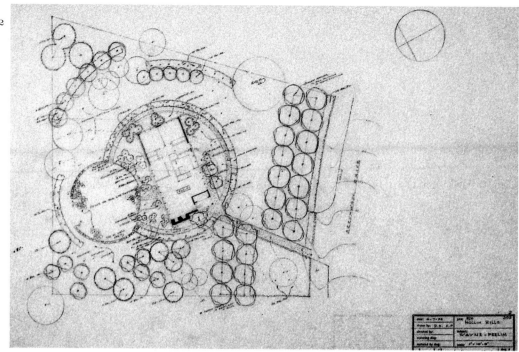

Wayne Garden, 7 June 1953 (FLL)

43

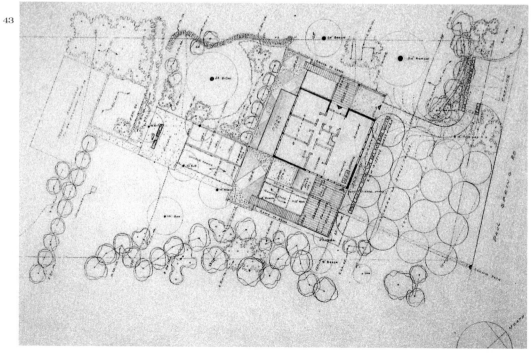

Mr. and Mrs. Adrienne Spivack Garden, 6 August 1953 (FLL)

# DAN KILEY'S MILLER GARDEN

Coming to Light

Gary R. Hilderbrand

Dan Kiley's Miller Garden in Columbus, Indiana (figs. 44–7) is considered a masterwork in the long span of Kiley's career, and indeed among the entire body of modernist landscape works of the mid-twentieth century. It figures prominently in discussions of modernism in landscape, notably those of Jory Johnson and Felice Frankel in *Modern Landscape Architecture: Redefining the Garden* and the collection of essays *Modern Landscape Architecture: A Critical Review*, edited by Marc Treib.[1] The words "Miller Garden" have assumed a kind of currency in discussions of landscape design, proof of this work's place as a standard by which other modern works may be evaluated.

Although the Miller Garden was designed and built from 1955 through 1958, its recognition as a modernist icon is a recent phenomenon. My aim here is to situate the design community's reception of the Miller Garden as a significant rediscovery during a period of change in landscape architecture's critical culture.[2] For over twenty years after it was built, the Miller project was little known; as a specimen of residential landscape design, it held little interest for the study of mainstream landscape architecture in the 1960s and 1970s, which had shifted its concerns to broader environmental issues, planning agendas, and suburbanization. The sudden popularity of the Miller Garden in the 1980s was instrumental in the reemergence of the residential landscape as a fundamental part of landscape architecture's everyday practice and its heritage.

Students of the modern landscape have come to know the Miller Garden principally through photographs—especially those taken first by Alan Ward in 1978—that have appeared in print in a number of publications. Because Irwin and Xenia Miller are intensely private about their home, in spite of their tremendous beneficence in Columbus and elsewhere, few outsiders have been granted access to their home and garden, even though everyone passes it during an architectural pilgrimage to Columbus. But we all know the Miller Garden through photographs and published plans—if that is a way of knowing it.

Kiley's project for the Millers, undertaken in 1955 after several years of work on the house by Eero Saarinen, was first published in 1958 in *Architectural Forum* and illustrated with photographs by the period's most notable architectural photographer, Ezra Stoller. The house

1. Jory Johnson and Felice Frankel, *Modern Landscape Architecture: Redefining the Garden* (New York: Abbeville Press, 1991); and Marc Treib, ed., *Modern Landscape Architecture: A Critical Review* (Cambridge, MA: MIT Press, 1993).

2. Portions of this discussion have appeared in my introductory essay "Photographing the Designed Landscape: A Practice of Seeing and Knowing," in Alan Ward, *Designed American Landscapes: A Photographic Interpretation* (Washington: Spacemaker Press, 1997), 6–7.

was cited by the editors for its resemblance to the quadrilateral symmetry and programmatic disposition of Andrea Palladio's sixteenth-century Villa Rotonda, albeit abstracted and asymmetrically organized within the confines of a large, low roof. The article, "A Contemporary Palladian Villa," is surprising in its explicit reference to such a precedent during the period.[3] Although the reading of the house as a villa is simplistic, its syntactical resemblance is evidence of Saarinen's interest in the pursuit of classical ordering tendencies within the modernist vocabulary. However, little was said of the garden. The project was also published a year later, in 1959, as *House & Garden's* "Hallmark House Number 3."[4] This article, "A New Concept of Beauty," emphasized a tame kind of domesticated modernism in the interior spaces and their decoration. Again, the garden was not a focus. And no other publication that I can find discusses the Miller Garden for at least twenty more years.

Certainly a number of academics and practitioners knew of the Miller Garden through direct contact with Kiley—although Kiley managed to remain at arm's length, always working outside the mainstream landscape architecture community. He did not mind *visiting* Harvard on occasion, but he did not want to be associated with it. He was his own network. Perhaps the only means of disseminating knowledge about the Miller Garden from 1959 through the late seventies was the infrequent appearance of Kiley himself at various schools and departments of landscape architecture around the country—Berkeley, Harvard, Penn, and elsewhere. Although he always spoke about the Miller Garden and has often described it as his first really modern project, it was the larger projects of the Jefferson National Expansion Memorial Competition in St. Louis, the Air Force Academy in Colorado Springs, and, later, Dulles Airport that most interested his audiences.[5] Stuart Dawson, a long-time Kiley acquaintance, has said that in 1957, when Kiley spoke to students at the University of Illinois, they were astonished and thrilled with Kiley's project for the Air Garden at the United States Air Force Academy—and not much interested in a residential project in nearby Indiana.[6]

So after its initial exposure as an architectural event, modest as it was, the Miller project enjoyed a quiet obscurity—it was generally not included in published discussions of Kiley's

3. "A Contemporary Palladian Villa," *Architectural Forum* 109 no. 3 (September 1958): 126–31.
4. "A New Concept of Beauty," *House & Garden* (February 1959): 58–71.
5. Interview with Dan Kiley, Charlotte, Vermont, September 1997.
6. Interview with Stuart Dawson, Watertown, Massachusetts, October 1997. Before attending Harvard Dawson received his BFA in landscape architecture from the University of Illinois in 1957.

work. Even the Museum of Modern Art's important 1964 book, *Modern Gardens and the Landscape,* by Elizabeth Kassler, did not include the Miller project.[7] Although Kiley was prolific during this period, his only projects featured in Kassler's book were the 1954 Air Force Academy and Independence Mall in Philadelphia. In fact, Kassler's inclusion of residential gardens in the show was modest, generally limited to exotic international abstractions (such as those by Roberto Burle Marx and Luis Barragan) or the somewhat radical—radical for New York, that is—California modernism of Thomas Church, Garret Eckbo, and Lawrence Halprin.

Among the reasons for the relative obscurity of the garden at mid-century was the emerging focus on planning and environmental design. Peter Walker and Melanie Simo, among others, have written about the tendency of landscape architecture at the time to identify with planning and design that was driven by a heightened sense of social and environmental concerns.[8] With an urgent and somewhat strident conviction about its role in environmental rescue, landscape architecture found a defining and legitimizing territory that purposely excluded the garden—the singular residential site—as relatively trivial. Surely the late 1930s writings of Christopher Tunnard, and later those of Lawrence Halprin, John Simonds, and Ian McHarg—and indeed Eckbo, Kiley, and James Rose in the 1930s—had helped to drive professionals toward larger scales of work and greater potential impact, and had at the same time brought into question the production of works involving wealthy patrons and immense personal resources. Ironically, landscape architecture's increased commitment to social purpose meant in theory a spirited and potent focus on the garden as a metaphor for all scales of environmental design, but, in practice, effectively a burial of the garden. In time, the garden receded from view.

Contemporary literature, both professional and popular, attests to this bias. A study of *Landscape Architecture Quarterly* over the years 1950 to 1960, the decade of Kiley's design of the Miller Garden and numerous other residential commissions, reveals that the discussion of gardens was virtually nonexistent, save for the occasional review of historic European or Asian sites.[9] *California Arts & Architecture,* bridging the professional culture and the shelter magazine market, may be the rare exception to this exclusivity. In California, it would seem, the garden

7. Elizabeth Kassler, *Modern Gardens and the Landscape* (New York: Museum of Modern Art, 1964).

8. Peter Walker and Melanie Simo, *Invisible Gardens: The Search for Modernism in the American Landscape* (Cambridge, MA: MIT Press, 1994). See especially the introduction and Chapter 9.

9. I thank Allyson Mendenhall for having the patience to search ten years of *Landscape Architecture* magazine. Little of any deep interest surfaced with respect to the garden.

did have social purpose—as Marc Treib and others have discussed—and never quite left land-scape architects' portfolios.[10] But on the whole, landscape architects who built residential works during this period were published only in the popular garden press, especially *House Beautiful*, *House & Garden*, and *Sunset* magazines.

Not everyone abandoned the garden in this period; to be sure, scholars are busy now opening up its history and bringing forward a more complex picture. But we can attribute the relative obscurity of Kiley's residential efforts at least partly to the vain fear the landscape architecture profession had of being identified with the scale of the residential garden and its perceived irrelevance and lack of social purpose. This insecurity lasted until the late 1970s.

The emergence of the Miller Garden as Kiley's masterwork and as an icon of mid-century American modernist residential space occurred during a resurgence of interest in the garden that began to gain momentum at the end of the seventies. In a little-known but prescient exhibition curated in 1980 by Peter Walker at Harvard University, entitled "Dan Kiley: Classicist in the Modern Landscape," Alan Ward exhibited large-format black-and-white prints of the Miller project. Four years later, a more substantial exhibition curated by Michael Van Valkenburgh, known as "Built Landscapes: Gardens in the Northeast," brought Kiley's Miller Garden forward in the context of other designs by Beatrix Farrand, Fletcher Steele, James Rose, and A. E. Bye.[11] The "Classicist" show left no permanent evidence, but Van Valkenburgh's "Built Landscapes" was influential. Its importance has been underestimated. The show traveled extensively in the United States and Canada for three years. The catalog was widely distrib-uted in two printings, and the exhibition received a national award from the American Society of Landscape Architects. "Built Landscapes" exemplified a renewed interest in the scale, craft, spatial vocabularies, and meanings in the designed garden. Alan Ward's images of the Miller Garden focused on the calm and careful order of Kiley's planted forms, the implicitly relaxed cadence of strolling spaces, the delicate transparency across the boundaries between house and site, and the synchrony of organization of garden spaces in relation to the mass and void of Saarinen's house. Finally, these qualities appealed to landscape architects.

10. See in particular Marc Treib, ed., *An Everyday Modernism: The Houses of William Wurster* (Berkeley: University of California Press, 1995); and Marc Treib and Dorothée Imbert, *Garret Eckbo: Modern Landscapes for Living* (Berkeley: University of California Press, 1997).

11. See the catalog to the exhibition, Michael Van Valkenburgh, *Built Landscapes: Gardens in the Northeast* (Brattleboro, VT: Brattleboro Museum and Art Center, 1984), 50–7.

Other events and trends by the early 1980s augured the return to the garden. For one, the controversy surrounding editor Grady Clay's decision to place Martha Schwartz's Bagel Garden on the cover of *Landscape Architecture* magazine in 1979 suggested a readiness for some—and a deep resistance by many—for the possibility of the garden as a legitimate site for building *or* for discourse (the resistance was not, I think, aimed at the use of bagels, but at the elevation of a simple garden of any kind to cover status). There was also controversy surrounding Stephen Krog's 1981 essay in *Landscape Architecture*, "Is it Art?," which assailed landscape architecture's intellectual reticence and pleaded for serious dialogue and for cultural relevance in design.[12] Moreover, teaching and scholarship in landscape architecture departments began to lean toward an art-historical, art-criticism kind of discourse. And this could *only* lead directly to the garden, where the issues of associative meaning, derivation from precedent, individual artistic practice, and site specificity could be shown to have the longest possible lineage. I would cite only one of the most visible of these efforts in schools, namely the analytical studies of garden, site, and architecture at the University of Virginia. With the encouragement of their dean, architect Jaquelin Robertson, faculty at Charlottesville pursued the garden rigorously, from the late 1970s on, through drawing, modeling, and field studies in both Virginia and Italy. Their persistence in restoring the garden's place in the curriculum, and, by implication, in practice, brought about an important public discussion of Kiley's work in 1982; the publicized proceedings of these discussion helped to secure Kiley's work as key to the garden's redemption and enabled the Miller Garden to come to prominence.[13]

Since its emergence as an important work, surprisingly few writers or critics have attempted to articulate its value with any precision. Gregg Bleam has made the most serious effort to do so in his essay "The Work of Dan Kiley."[14] Bleam situates the Miller Garden on the one hand within Kiley's own emerging concerns for space and order over a decade of diverse projects in the late 1940s and early 1950s and, on the other hand, within a larger modernist spatial agenda in Europe and America—informed partly by the lessons of space in De Stijl painting, by what he calls a neoclassical spatial motive, and by the decentralized and irregular

---

12. Stephen Krog, "Is it Art?," *Landscape Architecture* 71 no. 3 (May 1981): 373–6. Letters of protest (and a few of support) followed for several months in the magazine.

13. The University of Virginia's teaching and scholarship in this area was featured in a series of studies collectively entitled "House-and-Garden" in *Landscape Architecture* 73 no. 2 (March/April 1983). In particular, Elizabeth Meyer's "The Modern Framework" and Warren T. Byrd, Jr.'s "Comparative Anatomy: Donnell Garden & Dumbarton Oaks" brought forward discussions of garden morphology, the roots of modernism, and relationships to garden precedent. Dean Jaquelin Robertson, chair Harry Porter, faculty members Byrd and Reuben Rainey, and David Streatfield and Laurie Olin participated in the colloquium on Kiley's work. The proceedings, *The Work of Dan Kiley: A Dialogue on Design Theory*, edited by Byrd and Rainey (Charlottesville: University of Virginia, 1982), stand as an important reflection of design discourse in this period. Teachers at other institutions deserve mention for their leanings toward the garden in these years as well: Cherie Kluesing, Michael Van Valkenburgh, and Peter Walker at Harvard; Terry Harkness at Illinois; Robert Reich at LSU; Olin, then at Penn. The list is far longer.

14. Gregg Bleam, "Modern and Classical Themes in the Work of Dan Kiley," in Treib, *Modern Landscape Architecture*, 220–39.

organization of space in Mies van der Rohe's German Pavilion at Barcelona. Other discussions of the Miller Garden since Van Valkenburgh's first are either brief or uncritical, mostly as short notations in collections of Kiley projects, such as the *Process Architecture* series, or in surveys of modern landscape architecture projects, such as Jory Johnson and Felice Frankel's of 1991.[15]

Though the Miller Garden did not immediately draw attention from the landscape architecture community, Kiley's pursuit of modernism there amounted to a near catharsis. In his quest for transparency—the phenomenon of seeing and experiencing fluidly across the boundaries between architecture and landscape—Kiley cemented Saarinen's house to its site, grounding the landscape physically and perceptually, within direct reach of the interior spaces. The Millers' flat and open twelve-acre site afforded him a freedom of organization without hierarchy and without the kind of figuration familiar in traditional garden plans. This freedom allowed Kiley to focus on familiar planted forms—hedges, orchards, allées, and simple rows—with unencumbered freshness, and it gave him opportunities for abstraction and invention. Here Kiley's unabashed love for plants and how they could be used in space came through with great force, and because the garden was well maintained, they survived into maturity. Further, Kiley took up these modernist tendencies as a mutual pursuit with an architect whose sensibilities and convictions were similar to his own. Indeed, Kiley and Saarinen shared an affinity for a questioning and probing practice, and they forged a mutual respect and trust for each other's production.

In "Coming of Age: Eero Saarinen and Modern American Architecture," Peter Papademetriou points out that, especially during the 1950s, Saarinen's "questioning modernism" entailed rigorous research—through his built work—on the tectonics, the means of production, and the forms that could support new kinds of space for institutions and industry.[16] During the early and mid-1950s, Saarinen combined familiar precedents with emerging structural and technical solutions on many projects, including the General Motors Technical Center in Detroit, the IBM Manufacturing Facilities in Rochester and Research Facilities in Yorktown Heights, and Bell Laboratories in Holmdel, New Jersey, as well as science buildings for a number of univer-

15. Michiko Yamada, ed., *Dan Kiley: Landscape Design 2: In Step With Nature* (Tokyo: Process Architecture, 1993); Johnson and Frankel, *Modern Landscape Architecture*.

16. Peter Papademetriou, "Coming of Age: Eero Saarinen and Modern American Architecture," *Perspecta* 21 (New York: Yale University and Rizzoli International Publications, 1984): 116–43.

sities—and later, the air terminals at Kennedy Airport in New York and Dulles Airport in Washington. Saarinen's search for meaningful tectonic expression essentially defines his concerns as both technical and humanist, including both the precise abstraction and impeccable mechanics of steel production at General Motors and the rousing emotion in the gesture and form of concrete extrusion at the TWA Terminal. While Kiley's production was certainly smaller, and his passion for design as a reconciling and researching kind of work was less known, he certainly shared a conviction about the liberating force of modernity.

A second aspect of Kiley and Saarinen's collaboration is less certain and more elusive, but no less apparent: their wry independence from the intellectual burdens of their fields and their conviction that design and life are inseparable. Saarinen pursued design through dichotomous and overlapping motivations: informed by the needs of production of large-scale industrial buildings, he perfected a corporate enterprise that was able to produce several major buildings at the same time; yet, equally important, he drew on his Scandinavian traditions and his parents' love of building, their devotion to craft and local practices of making, and their respect for traditional forms as a basis of knowledge and repository of cultural meaning. Kiley turned his disdain for what he perceived as an outdated, falsely aristocratic resistance to modernity in his profession into a highly modern life for himself and his family in rural New England: a deliberate separation from the city (not a suburban semidetachment) that required long-distance motoring and air travel before either was fashionable or comfortable, and a partially decentralized family life among a number of dwellings and pavilions dispersed on a large piece of Vermont woodland—enabling a workaholic life without the complete abandonment of familial responsibility. In Charlotte, business, travel, recreation, and family life intersected to a significant extent. With all this, an unusually calm and robustly confident designer attracted partners, collaborators, and clients to come in legendary numbers to this remote center. It must have appealed a great deal to Saarinen, and to many others as well. Go there today, and you inevitably sense the completeness and sereneness of life that enabled Kiley to sustain his practice and his search, and that created desire in others to be near it.

Let me relate these characteristics to the Miller Garden. Kiley and Saarinen shaped their work with an unerring sense of modernity's impacts on ways of living and the space of living, but counter to the prevailing accusations of historical amnesia for the period, neither Saarinen nor Kiley worked in denial of the precedents that could be adapted for modern living. Devout modernist that he is, Kiley has said that he did not make *conscious* references to precedent, and one is inclined to believe him, but knowledge of and respect for traditions surely are present in much of his work. He speaks, for example, of André Le Nôtre and of the influence of agriculture. And he says that Saarinen did not make explicit use of precedents either, but that, of course, his foundation of knowledge of architectural history was never far from his deliberations over form and technology.[17] Saarinen's regularly ordered structural system for the Miller House has traces of the central planning and hierarchical space of classical pavilions, and it pursues a refinement of the structural expression that he had sought in several earlier projects. Kiley, identified by some as one of the rebels who rejected history, never did so. Rather, he rejected the pompous intellectual authority and tired formal manners of his teachers and the elite of his profession. He wanted a modern sensibility, especially toward the simple organization of space for function and visual beauty. Both nature and history enabled this sensibility.

In the Miller project, the shared motivations of the designers conspired in the making of a precisely ordered house and grounds. Yet another fact about the house is interesting: if Kiley's project for Miller suffered obscurity because of professional bias, Saarinen's house has remained even more obscure, after its initial publication in 1958 and 1959. To this day, the major publications on Saarinen's work—even Allan Temko's comprehensive study—avoid any reference to the Miller House.[18] It is likely that the Millers' desire for privacy, still closely guarded, made it difficult for scholars to gain access. Perhaps also the house has been thought anomalous—indeed, one may regard it almost as a garden pavilion—among Saarinen's giants of corporate elegance and technological prowess. Still, as landscape architects gradually overcame their mistrust of the garden, the fruits of a collaboration like that of Saarinen and Kiley, even at this scale, became plausibly interesting.

17. Interview with Kiley.
18. Allan Temko, *Eero Saarinen* (New York: George Braziller, 1962).

A detailed description of the garden is not possible here; it is the subject of another study.[19] Yet however we might describe the Miller Garden, in order to understand and acclaim its importance and its beauty, this much is clear: in landscape architecture's belated, deliberative search for its own modernity (which is a continuing struggle), the Miller Garden is there to fill the void as its most enduring icon. Kiley's work, appearing as it did during the nascent development of a new kind of scholarship and during a revival of landscape architecture's most ancient and noble form of expression—the garden—demanded to be understood and appreciated. A small but growing number of critics and teachers were willing to make a case for it. Because it had remained little known for over twenty years, it reached a kind of maturity of growth and habit that made it instantly palpable and spatially complex, even in photographs. By the time the photographs appeared, it was as if Kiley's garden had had no infancy—something with which landscapes always struggle. Its absolutely impeccable condition, fostered by a level of caring maintenance unmatched almost anywhere, gave us a sense of the modern landscape as finely crafted artifice, and in this we had something of a newly legitimizing claim for the field. The Miller Garden filled the void so well that Michael Van Valkenburgh could not resist including it in his modest compilation of so-called *Gardens of the Northeast* in 1984.[20] Far from the east or the north, the garden is in Indiana. But how on earth could he leave this out?

In the Miller Garden, Kiley shaped a modern space imbued with transparency and complexity, and delicately balanced between tension and freedom. He achieved this through mutual purposes with a driven architect, and also through his own singular sense of the demands and the pleasures of modern living. In Saarinen's house, we see an intellectual and analytical modern space, a space so strenuously in pursuit of the most inspired tectonic craft of its time that it became not a great work of architecture but an elegant period piece. The house is beautifully dated. But in the garden, we see a timeless space that is modern but not fixed to a moment in the modernist chronology, not polemical, not totalizing, not even formally resolved—just intelligently and softly juxtaposed. Once discovered—really rediscovered—the careful order and calm spatial syntax of Kiley's work at the Miller Garden appealed to those

19. See "The Miller Garden: Icon of Modernity," in Gary R. Hilderbrand, *The Miller Garden: Icon of Modernism* (Washington, D.C.: Spacemaker Press, 1999).

20. Van Valkenburgh, *Built Landscapes*.

who wished to have the garden return to the center of landscape architecture's domain. Unlike so many landscape architects who charged themselves with modernism's great challenges, Kiley never abandoned the garden. He always believed in it. And it was this, his most beautiful project, that restored our faith in designing domestic landscape space. For a younger generation ready to acclaim both modernist and postmodern sensibilities in the garden, the open-ended geometries and spatial dissonances that we found customary by the mid-1980s were enabled by the discovery of the Miller Garden. Kiley's gentle upsetting of conventions ultimately loosened us from dependence on resolved geometries and overtly mannered devices; it also renewed our interest in the materials of landscape. In his hands, modern space became more than an abstraction of the series or the grid, more than an elaboration of pattern. In the process, the garden was restored to its rightful place as a sustaining vehicle for expression with precise—yet nearly infinite—possibilities for meaning.

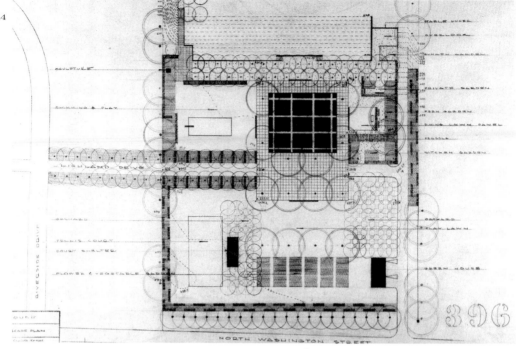

Site plan of Miller Garden, August 1955 (FLL)

View toward Henry Moore sculpture in the adult garden, 1997 (Gary R. Hilderbrand)

View of Honeylocust Allée, 1997 (Gary R. Hilderbrand)

Honeylocust Allée and meadow, 1997 (Gary R. Hilderbrand)

Checklist of drawings from the Special Collections, Frances Loeb
Library, Harvard University, exhibited at Dan Kiley: The First Two
Decades, November 1997, Joseph Disponzio, curator. (Job Number
refers to the master job list from the Office of Dan Kiley. It does not
necessarily signify chronology.)

18    Edward D. Hollander Residence, Washington, D.C.
      "Layout Plan," 4 August 1941
      "Planting Plan," 10 March 1942

19    Clark Foreman Residence, Washington, D.C.
      "Preliminary Sketch," 16 August 1941

30    Walter Bleakney Residence, Princeton, NJ
      "General Development Plan," 27 February 1942
      "Construction Details," 6 March 1942

33    Frederic W. Beckman Residence, Princeton, NJ
      "House Area Plan," 20 March 1942
      "General Development Plan," 22 March 1942
      "House Area Planting Plan," 16 April 1942

42    Lilly Ponds Houses, Washington, D.C.
      "Landscape Site Plan," blueprint, 22 October 1942

138   McCall's Magazine
      [Backyard plans, 1948]

155   Hamilton Residence, Princeton, NJ
      "Plot Layout," 4 April 1949
      "Landscape Plan," 2 May 1949
      "Shelter Details," 14 July 1949
      "Planting Details and Revisions," 9 November 1949

172   Dr. Barnet Fine Residence, Stanford, CT
      "Construction and Grading Plan," 10 July 1950
      "Planting Plan," 14 July 1950
      "Construction Details," 17 July 1950
      "Site Development—Pond," 14 September 1950

185   L. C. Baker Residence, Greenwich, CT
      "General Site Plan," 18 October 1950
      "General Master Plan," 18 December 1950
      "Planting Plan," 14 January 1950
      "Shelter, Pools, Screens," 3 March 1951

189   Living Magazine. Site Planning Article, [1951]
      [Planting and Layout Plan]
      [Site Plan]

190   Kenneth Kassler Prototype. House #2, Princeton, NJ
      "Prototype Garden #1," 30 June 1950

191   Richard S. Gile Residence, Midland, TX
      "Preliminary [Layout Plan]," [1951]

205   Mr. and Mrs. Rudolph Talbot Residence, Hingham, MA
      "Preliminary Landscape Sketch," 13 June 1951
      "General Planting Plan," 8 August 1951
      [Location and Plot Plan, n.d.]

239   Richardson Dwellings, Washington, D.C.
      "Location Plan East," sepia print, 27 May 1952
      "Landscape Plan East," sepia print, 27 May 1952
      "Location Plan West," sepia print, 27 May 1952
      "Landscape Plan West," sepia print, 27 May 1952

363   Henry Stokes Residence, Hingham, MA
      "Preliminary Sketch," 12 April 1954
      "Planting Plan," 7 October 1954

396   Irwin and Xenia Miller Residence, Columbus, IN
      "Preliminary Landscape Plan," August 1955
      "Plant Bloom Period, March–April," 3 September 1957
      "Plant Bloom Period, May–June," 3 September 1957
      "Planting Plan. North Garden," 16 December 1957
      "Entrance Area and East Lawn," 31 July 1957

398   Concordia Senior College, Fort Wayne, IN
      "Preliminary Planting Design," 4 December 1955
      "General Site Plan," 5 December 1955
      "Administration Area, Preliminary Planting Design,"
      5 December 1955
      "Faculty Housing Area, Preliminary Planting Design,"
      6 December 1955

415   United States Air Force Academy, Colorado Springs, CO
      [Schematic Design, Cadet Quadrangle Gardens and Air
      Gardens, n.d.]
      "Landscaping Cadet Academic Area," blueprint [n.d.]
      "Planting Plan, Quadrangle Garden," blueprint [n.d.]

434   Richard Davis Residence, Wayzata, MN
      "Preliminary Landscape Plan," 15 July 1958

457   Independence Mall, Philadelphia, PA
      [Volumetric Analysis (Axonometric Drawing), n.d.]
      [Preliminary Sketch Design, n.d.]
      [Schematic Development Plan, n.d.]
      [Preliminary Sketch Design, n.d.]
      [Layout Plan, n.d.]
      [Layout with Plants Key, Planting Plan, n.d.]
      "Planting Details," blueprint, 1 December 1960

459   Stephen R. Currier Cottage, Danby, VT
      "Amended and Enlarged Planting Plan" 27 October 1959

Hollin Hills drawings exhibited at Dan Kiley: The First Two Decades, listed chronologically

"Unit House, no. 2": blueprint plot plan, 23 March 1949

251/270: Model #206. "Planting Plan," 5 May 1953

209/272: Wayne Residence. "Preliminary Site Plan," 7 June 1953

276: R. Scott Moore Residence. "Planting Plan," 31 July 1953

215/279: Mr. and Mrs. Raymond E. Odum Residence, "Planting Plan," 4 August 1953

266: Martin M. Rosen Residence. "Planting Plan," 5 August 1953

302: Mr. and Mrs. Adrienne Spivack Residence. "Planting Plan," 6 August 1953

269: Goodhue Residence. "Planting Plan," 10 August 1953

284: Edward Risley Residence. "Planting Plan," 12 August 1953

254: Medvin Residence. "Planting Plan," 30 August 1953

263: Daugherty Residence. "Planting Plan," 9 September 1953

291: Hill Residence. "Planting Plan," 12 September 1953

300: Jones Residence. "Planting Plan," 12 September 1953

260: Mr. and Mrs. Gordon Record Residence. "Planting Plan," 21 September 1953

307: Goding Residence. "Planting Plan," 24 September 1953

256: Mr. and Mrs. Vincent G. Macaluso Residence. "Planting Plan," 12 October 1953

294: J. R. Lane Residence. "Planting Plan," 8 December 1953

268: Johnson Residence. "Final Planting Plan," 10 December 1953

299: D. P. Hill Residence. "Entrance Ramp and Slide," 10 December 1953

317: Rogers Residence. "Final Planting Plan," 25 January 1955

257: Mr. and Mrs. Kenen Residence. "Planting Plan," 4 February 1954

290: Howard H. Wallace, Jr., Residence. "Planting Plan" 4 February 1954

318: Wallace Residence. 4 February 1954

285: G. H. Lorimer Residence. "Planting Plan," 4 March 1954

299: D. P. Hill Residence. "Final Planting Plan," 12 April 1954

289: Robert C. Vorhis Residence. "Final Planting Plan," 7 May 1954

308: S. L. Henderson Residence. "Final Planting Plan," 7 May 1954

288: J. W. Sayre Residence. "Final Planting Plan," 21 June 1954

327: E. F. Preston Residence. "Final Planting Plan," 29 June 1954

314: David P. Coffin Residence. "Final Planting Plan," 2 July 1954

315: Herbert Hubben Residence. "Final Planting Plan," 2 July 1954

329: Nathan Seeman Residence. "Final Planting Plan," 23 July 1954

310: Martin Rogin Residence. "Final Planting Plan," 17 August 1954

35009: Miller Residence. "Final Planting Plan," 3 November 1954

264: H. S. Klink Residence. "Final Planting Plan," 7 December 1954

265: John London Residence. "Final Planting Plan," 12 December 1954

305: Charles Feldman Residence. "Final Planting Plan," 15 December 1954

309: David G. West Residence. "Final Planting Plan," 19 December 1954

325: Mogin Residence. "Final Planting Plan," 1 January 1955

304: Odoroff Residence. "Final Planting Plan," 13 January 1955

301: R. M. Leighton Residence. "Final Planting Plan," 24 January 1955

320: Wald Residence. "Final Planting Plan," 2 February 1955

321: Buffmire Residence. "Final Planting Plan," 7 February 1955

322: Blooston Residence. "Final Planting Plan," 10 February 1955

324: Strelow Residence. "Final Planting Plan," 14 February 1955

306: Newsham Residence. "Final Planting Plan," 8 March 1955

340: Martin Residence. "Final Planting Plan," 6 May 1955

5005: Christie Residence. "Final Planting Plan," 7 May 1955

5007: Briggs Residence. "Final Planting Plan," 13 May 1955

390: Trimble Residence. "Final Planting Plan," 17 May 1955

334: D. C. Vorhis Residence. "Final Planting Plan," 27 June 1955

337: Evans Residence. "Final Planting Plan," 16 July 1955

339: Newfield Residence. "Final Planting Plan," 16 July 1955

5008: Michela Residence. "Final Planting Plan," 21 July 1955

Kiley himself has written very little. Still serviceable is his early essay "Nature: The Source of All Design," which appeared in *Landscape Architecture* (January 1963): 8–10. It is among the first—if not the first—articles by Kiley; curiously, his words preceded his designs in this professional journal. Another early source of his design philosophy is given in *Landmark* (Berkeley: University of California, 1965), 8–10. The University of Virginia symposium "The Work of Dan Kiley: A Dialogue on Design Theory—Proceedings of the First Annual Symposium on Landscape Architecture" (Charlottesville, 1982) is an early investigation of his work and remains important. Gregg Bleam's "The Work of Dan Kiley," in *Modern Landscape Architecture: A Critical Review*, ed. Marc Treib (Cambridge: MIT Press, 1993), 220–39, is less comprehensive in scope and critique than its title implies, but is nevertheless an important work of Kiley scholarship; it set a standard infrequently matched. *Process: Architecture 33. Landscape Design: Works of Dan Kiley* (Tokyo: Process Architecture, 1982) (with essays by Frederick Gutheim and Dan Kiley) and M. Yamada, ed., *Process: Architecture 108. Dan Kiley: Landscape Design II* (Tokyo: Process Architecture, 1993) (with texts by Kiley, Yoji Sasaki, Harry Wolf, and Jaquelin Robertson) are welcome and include significant visual material, but are not critical works. Sporadically, Kiley is treated in general works on modern landscape architecture, notably Mark Treib's "Axioms for a Modern Landscape Architecture" in *Modern Landscape Architecture* (36–67) and chapter 6 of Peter Walker and Melanie Simo's *Invisible Gardens: The Search for Modernism in the American Landscape* (Cambridge, MA: MIT Press, 1994). Caution must be taken when using architectural encyclopedia entries on Kiley. *Contemporary Architects* (London: St. James Press) rewrote its entry on Kiley between the second (1987) and third (1994) editions: Pauline Saliga's entry in the third edition is the better of the two. Many of these citations are sloppy in accounting something as elementary as dates. Two recent "retrospectives" in New York (Architectural League of New York, 1996) and London (Architecture Foundation, 1995) did not add to Kiley scholarship.